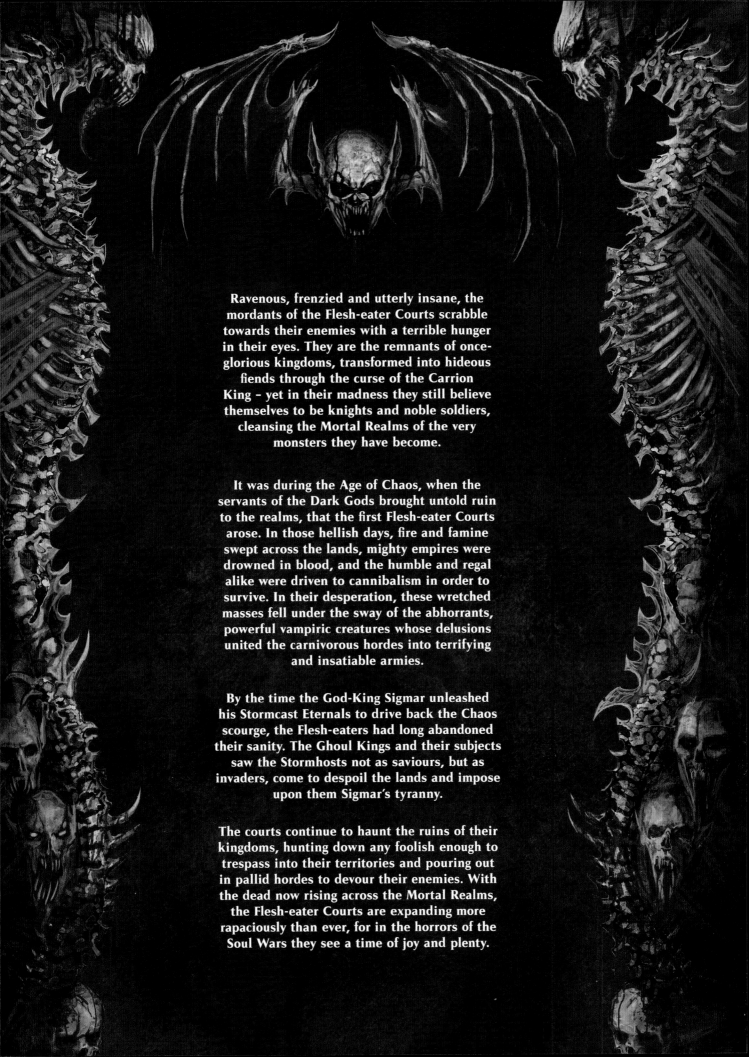

Ravenous, frenzied and utterly insane, the mordants of the Flesh-eater Courts scrabble towards their enemies with a terrible hunger in their eyes. They are the remnants of once-glorious kingdoms, transformed into hideous fiends through the curse of the Carrion King – yet in their madness they still believe themselves to be knights and noble soldiers, cleansing the Mortal Realms of the very monsters they have become.

It was during the Age of Chaos, when the servants of the Dark Gods brought untold ruin to the realms, that the first Flesh-eater Courts arose. In those hellish days, fire and famine swept across the lands, mighty empires were drowned in blood, and the humble and regal alike were driven to cannibalism in order to survive. In their desperation, these wretched masses fell under the sway of the abhorrants, powerful vampiric creatures whose delusions united the carnivorous hordes into terrifying and insatiable armies.

By the time the God-King Sigmar unleashed his Stormcast Eternals to drive back the Chaos scourge, the Flesh-eaters had long abandoned their sanity. The Ghoul Kings and their subjects saw the Stormhosts not as saviours, but as invaders, come to despoil the lands and impose upon them Sigmar's tyranny.

The courts continue to haunt the ruins of their kingdoms, hunting down any foolish enough to trespass into their territories and pouring out in pallid hordes to devour their enemies. With the dead now rising across the Mortal Realms, the Flesh-eater Courts are expanding more rapaciously than ever, for in the horrors of the Soul Wars they see a time of joy and plenty.

# CONTENTS

## DESIGNED BY GAMES WORKSHOP IN NOTTINGHAM
With thanks to The Faithful for their additional playtesting services.

Games Workshop Ltd., Willow Road, Lenton, Nottingham, NG7 2WS, United Kingdom
**games-workshop.com**

*As the pall of death spreads over the Mortal Realms, the deranged cannibals of the Flesh-eater Courts emerge from the ruins of once-great civilizations in search of prey.*

# CANNIBAL KINGDOMS

**Hidden among the ruins of the Mortal Realms are the Flesh-eater Courts. Bound by the madness of their cursed monarchs, throngs of creatures known as mordants eke out a wretched existence, waging wars against kingdom after kingdom in order to feast on the flesh of their enemies.**

Echoing through the mouldering rubble of once-magnificent kingdoms comes the sound of scrambling claws and the wet smack of blood-stained lips. At the centre of this horrific din stands an abhorrant, and in a voice that is at once regal and raving he sounds the call to war. As his snarled command reverberates across the ruins, scores of Crypt Ghouls come racing from their dens, remnants of recent meals still dripping from gaping mouths as they charge out to find fresh prey. Hulking Crypt Horrors lope ahead of the ghoul throngs, brandishing the bones of those they have devoured and bellowing gibbered commands. Overhead, the skies darken as Crypt Flayers and giant cadaverous beasts take wing, deafening those below with screeches and roars as they fly forth to hunt.

Wherever the Flesh-eaters gather, the air quickly grows thick with the reek of decaying meat, and the ground becomes littered with filth-encrusted bones. Yet the mordants do not see themselves as grotesque wretches – in their madness, they are instead gallant soldiers and noble knights, marching out in full regalia to conquer the wicked and rid the lands of evil. Born from the twisted mind of their abhorrant kings, this sorcerous delusion stays with them even as they rip the flesh from their enemies' bones with their bare teeth.

### DRIVEN TO DEPRAVITY
In every corner of the realms, nightmarish tales are told of the Flesh-eater Courts. When war and famine ravage a land, its most desperate and determined people survive in any way they can. Giving in to hunger, they turn upon the fallen, the weak, and even each other in their quest for sustenance. Retreating into the shadowed ruins of their towns and cities, these cannibal cults devolve into hideous parodies of society, kept alive on a

diet of rancid flesh and bone. Even then these creatures are worthy of pity, for their transformation into ghouls is not yet complete; only once they partake of an abhorrant king's feast do they become what are known as mordants.

The kings themselves are bestial vampires who rule over swathes of the Mortal Realms by the strength of their ragged courts. Completely delusional, they have become known as abhorrants by their soulblighted kin. Abhorrant Ghoul Kings are so lost in their madness that they believe themselves to be mortal monarchs, while Abhorrant Archregents perceive themselves as emperors ruling over vast domains. When they come to a place infested with cannibals, they see not monsters, but starving peasants and soldiers eager for the hand of a beneficent master. Each abhorrant is more than just a delusional beast – they are also the source of contagious madness. Weak minds are quickly

turned, but even the strong-willed soon see the king as he sees himself. Before long, those that once hid in shame from the light stand tall, armoured in delusion. In a mockery of civilisation, the abhorrant brings them into his court, inviting the pale horrors that bow and scrape in his presence to join in his grisly feasts.

By the will of the abhorrants do the courts congregate in the realms. Gathering up feasts from among the living and the dead, they rend apart their enemies and prepare the flesh of the fallen for their lord's culinary pleasure. Some mordants might even be blessed to sup the king's blood – in their minds drinking wine from their master's table. However, the thick crimson draught brings with it a terrifying transformation. These creatures arise as drooling horrors, slaved utterly to their new master, and bereft of what remained of their sanity. In time, a few of these 'blessed' ones might even ascend from mordants to join the vampire ranks of the abhorrants, and if fortune favours them, in turn found their own courts, thus spreading the madness of the Flesh-eaters.

### DESOLATE DOMAINS
Mordants lurk amid the ruins of countless fallen empires, their depraved nations bound together by a shared madness. As the abhorrant kings who rule over these fallow kingdoms grow in power, so too do their mockeries of civilisation slowly spread their sinister influence further across the realms.

By the beginning of the Age of Sigmar, the Flesh-eaters thrived in dark corners across the Mortal Realms. For centuries beyond count the abhorrants had followed the heady scent of battle, claiming for themselves places to raise their banners and form their courts amidst the mayhem of war. It was these ghoulish migrations that

seeded courts from the Dreaming Tombs of Hysh and the great Oakbastions of Ghyran to the Quicksilver Vales of Chamon and Themacarn Wastes of Aqshy. On the Penumbral Sea of Ulgu, floating kingdoms are filled with countless mordant shadows, while the Splinterbridge cities of Shyish's carrion deltas groan under the weight of corpulent cannibals. Outside of Azyr, there are few lands within the Mortal Realms that do not conceal a court. As mortal, daemon and undead armies storm through Realmgates or march across continents to war, the Flesh-eaters often go to battle both with and against them.

Many courts have made their homes around Realmgates, learning that these are places of battle and riches, and the nearby lands are always ripe for bloody harvests. Often, an invader will have no knowledge that they are walking into a domain claimed by an abhorrant until the ruins around them come alive with a thousand sets of hungry eyes.

Utilising the sorcery of these gates, there also exist sprawling Flesh-eater alliances. Kings and their courts, having divided up portions of the realms, use the gates to connect their ruinous lands. Some of the largest of these confederations even span multiple realms, like the Wargspine Citadel Grand Court. Amidst the vast ruin of this once-great fortification, countless courts have arisen to infest the castle's great bastions, each of which exists in a different realm. Wargspine is a stronghold many foes have tried to claim, though all have failed.

From the perspective of the abhorrants, the other races are usurpers and invaders. Unholy barbarians hammer at their gates and slay their subjects, and thus deserve only death. After all, it is the duty of a good king to watch over his people and keep them from harm.

No matter how far the mordants and their abhorrant kings spread throughout the realms, their wretched presence always draws the gaze of Nagash. The Lord of Death has long held plans for the Flesh-eaters. Despite the strange place they occupy, being neither fully living nor truly dead, Nagash considers them his own, and there has been a shadowy struggle fought between the Flesh-eaters and their deathless god over the centuries. Some have journeyed to the Realm of Death to kneel before the necromancer, their kings cowed by the Death God's might. Many, however, have purposefully put distance between themselves and their would-be overlord, fearful of the revenge the God of Death might visit upon them.

---

*K*ing Pergrin looked down into the valley before him, surveying the hovels and gore-filled trenches of the enemy encampment. Writhing amongst the filth and squalor he saw the pallid bodies of his foe – wretched creatures all, devoid of mercy and any semblance of civility. He had long pursued these monstrosities. Having driven them from his lands after years of their predations against his subjects, he had hounded them into their squalid realm, slaughtering them without restraint so that his kingdom might at last be free of their curse. Now but a single band of them remained, not more than five hundred in number, and he had them cornered in the valley below. Soon they would be no more, and the nightmare they had brought to his people would finally be over.

Pergrin raised his sword arm high, then glanced over his shoulder at the gleaming ranks of armoured soldiers behind him.

'Show them no mercy!' he bellowed.

The soldiers advanced as one. Infantrymen poured over the crest of the hill in crisp rows, moving swiftly yet with precision fit for a parade ground. Alongside them rode the knights of the domain, their flapping banners proudly displaying the colours of every fief in the kingdom. With his army in full advance, Pergrin pressed his heels into his mount, signalling to the griffon that it was time to fly into battle. The magnificent beast launched itself into the air, and with

a powerful beat of its wings began soaring forwards, over the heads of the soldiers below, down the ridge towards the wretched enemy.

'Show them no mercy!' Pergrin shouted again, his impassioned voice carrying over the clatter of arms and armour. His loyal troops replied in kind, their battle cry echoing across the valley…

Kastor Veldan, last general of the Sapphire Kingdoms, heard the inhuman snarling filtering down into the valley. He reached for his scabbard and rushed out of his tent, wearily trying to recall how many troops he still had after the last engagement. Whatever the number, it would not be enough. Emerging through the tent folds, the general saw the few remnants of his once-grand army forming up for a last defence. Their bravery could not be denied, even now, when all hope had been dashed.

Veldan looked beyond his troops and saw the endless swarm of Ghouls and Crypt Horrors pouring down the ridge towards them. Flying above them upon an undead monstrosity was the leader, the Ghoul King who had hunted the people of the Sapphire Kingdoms to extinction. Veldan knew that soon he and his soldiers would be gone too, his flesh ripped from his bones and devoured by the mad throng of the enemy. He knew this, yet he drew his sword, stood beside his troops, and prepared to die with honour.

The armies of the courts surge into battle to the sound of insane howling and bellowed gibberish. But as the slaughter wears on, and fear and madness start to take hold, the enemy begin to share in the insanity, hearing the silver trumpets and rousing speeches that echo in the minds of the cannibals.

# THE CARRION KING

**From ancient vampire bloodlines were the original abhorrant kings spawned. Shunned by their kin for their cannibalistic ways, they scattered out into the realms, weaving trails of madness through the ruins left by the Age of Chaos and becoming the first generation of Abhorrant Ghoul Kings.**

The origins of the abhorrants are an ancient and tragic tale. During the Age of Myth, the first abhorrant roamed the realms. He had been a favoured servant of Nagash, and back then he was fair and strong, and was surrounded by a loyal court of knights and nobles. Wherever he travelled, he administered justice in the name of the Great Necromancer, building hallowed shrines dedicated to the worship of the God of Death and glorious mausoleums where departed ancestors could be given their due. He also helped the weak and infirm pass into the underworlds, and took life from tyrants who misused their mortal existence. Before becoming the first abhorrant, this champion was known by many names in many lands – Sumeros Summerking, the Blood Rose Prince and Ushoran the Handsome to name but a few – and he was equally loved and feared. Those civilisations that paid their due to Nagash welcomed his coming, and lined their streets with graverose petals as he walked among them, whereas those who usurped the natural order of life and death were made to feel the full measure of his wrath.

Though the truth of his ignominious decline has been lost to the march of time, it is believed by many that the king fell out of favour with Nagash and was punished with a hideous transformation. No longer was he welcomed as a benevolent saviour; instead he was shunned and even hunted by those empires for whom he had done so much. Malformed and filled with anger against his former master, he became a monster like no other, and began prowling the Nightlands of Shyish. He continued to travel from land to land, but instead of granting boons to the Great Necromancer's loyal subjects, he offered them only a portion of his bitter malice. Such was the devastation spread by his fury that scores of Nagash's kingdoms were destroyed, their lords slain, their peoples torn apart and their cities reduced to naught but ruins and broken corpses.

Such an insult could not be borne by Nagash, and so he ordered his Mortarchs – most loyal and powerful of his servants – to bring the wayward king to heel. The Mortarchs of Night, Sacrament and Blood gathered their unliving armies, and in a series of brutal wars managed to scatter the last of the king's forces. The one known as Ushoran was brought before Nagash, but rather than obliterating his soul the Great Necromancer imprisoned his former servant in a prison called the Shroudcage. A towering edifice of broken promises, its walls reflected endless untruths upon the king, reducing him to a raving wreck, as twisted in mind as he was in body. So the king might have stayed for

all eternity, had not the God-King Sigmar descended from Azyr. In the first years of the Age of Chaos, Sigmar invaded the Realm of Death, incensed by Nagash's perceived betrayal at the Allpoints. During Sigmar's rampage through the Great Necromancer's domain, his armies brought down the bastion that held the Shroudcage, unwittingly allowing the thing that would become known as the Carrion King to scuttle forth from the ruin.

Loosed into the shadows, the first abhorrant began to build his court once more. He found those knights who had survived the wars against Nagash's Mortarchs – those who were still loyal to their sovereign lord – and upon them he bestowed a portion of his grand madness, before setting out to travel the lands once more. In his insanity, the Carrion King believed himself the benevolent champion he once had been, when in truth he had become more monstrous than ever. Cities of cowering mortals, tomb-fortresses of undead warriors and invading Chaos armies, all had the abhorrant's kindness visited upon them, and were left broken and butchered. The Carrion King found a willing source of servants amongst lost and depraved mortal cannibals – and in those times such wretches were plentiful indeed. With his blood he created sycophants to sing his praises from the foot of his dark throne, and many of these in turn went on to create their own courts. So it is that each Flesh-eater Court is a reflection of the First Court, their abhorrants trying to recreate in madness the memories passed on to them through blood.

It was during this same age that Nagash was laid low by Archaon, the Everchosen of the Chaos Gods. The Great Necromancer was not destroyed completely, and was spirited away by his Mortarchs to the underworld of Stygxx, there to slowly regain his sundered power. Nonetheless, in his absence the empire of the Carrion King expanded greatly. The abhorrants he created spread throughout Shyish before travelling through the Realmgates to found kingdoms in far-distant lands. Like all inhabitants of the Mortal Realms, these courts were set upon by the armies of the Dark Gods, but where most civilisations crumbled to dust under the relentless advance of Chaos, the Flesh-eaters thrived. For every army of mordants that were hacked apart or set ablaze by idolatrous warriors, more were raised from the pitiful masses that had been left to wither and die in the ruins of once-glorious cities. United by the madness of an abhorrant, these mordants turned their hunger into a deadly weapon.

During the Age of Chaos, when anarchy and ruination abounded, what few tales were told of the Carrion King came to an abrupt end. Though the influence of his derangement persisted and continued to grow, his whereabouts became completely unknown. More mysterious still are his motives and loyalties, for none can truly say whether the Carrion King continues to rage against Nagash, or if in his madness he believes himself to be in the Great Necromancer's good graces. Many of those courts descended from him fight alongside the undead armies of the Mortarchs, but others attack the servants of Nagash on sight. Those whose cursed lineage is least removed from the Carrion King still live within the ruins of his ancient kingdom deep within Shyish. In them, the curse of the king is strong, and their collective madness feeds off and permeates the land. The further from this ruinous empire the courts stray, the more their delusions diverge from that of the Carrion King, though the degree of their insanity remains undiminished.

The full truth of Ushoran's tale has been forgotten by all but one: the Great Necromancer. Indeed, Nagash remembers well what transpired, and still seeks his former champion across the Mortal Realms.

## THE FIRST COURT

Before his descent into madness, a court of knights and nobles followed Ushoran on his journeys. Drawn from different corners of the realms, this court comprised the finest and most noble of warrior lords, and together they rode resplendent as glorious children of the night. Some were peerless statesmen, entrusted by their liege to impart chivalry to the kingdoms to which they travelled. Others were mighty warlords, commanded to defend the meek and eradicate the unjust. These knights were still unshakeably devoted to their king, even after he had been afflicted by Nagash's curse, fighting alongside him as he waged war throughout Shyish. When the Mortarchs were sent to apprehend Ushoran, his court fought to the bitter end. Many died, others were scattered, yet even in defeat they remained loyal.

Some believe it was the knights of the court that lured Sigmar towards the stronghold where their liege was imprisoned. Freed from the Shroudcage, the Carrion King gathered those who had been his courtiers to his side once more, passing his insanity to them and making them the First Court in his resurrected empire. Lord Marrowbroth took up his position of old as protector of the Carrion King, gathering elite mordants to his ragged banner to ensure no harm would again befall the sovereign. The swift and secretive Baron Gizzard commanded Ghouls in great patrols around the borders of his lord's burgeoning lands, seeking out enemies who dared draw near and slaughtering any who let their guard down. These and others were the first of the Carrion King's cursed descendants, and they carved out a gruesome domain in Shyish during the Age of Chaos before spreading out into the realms to found new courts of their own. Of this initial generation of abhorrants, little else is known, their histories lost beneath a veil of time and madness. It is said that some travel the realms as Archregents, and that others fight beside the Carrion King to this day.

# COURTS OF DELUSION

**Just as in any mortal court, an abhorrant king's followers are each assigned a station under his beneficent rule. Lords and courtiers command soldiers, servants and peasants, with all mordants accepting their rank and role within the infectious madness of their masters.**

A sane observer looking upon a Flesh-eater Court sees only a nest of bestial cannibalism and mindless horror. Wretched Crypt Ghouls root around in piles of reeking dead, their filthy claws picking decaying meat from rancid bones while they snarl and spit at each other in a guttural tongue. Packs of towering Crypt Horrors, Haunters and their kin loom in the shadows like deathless guardians, darting into the press of ghouls to claim whole corpses at will. The mass of pallid bodies writhes like a cluster of maggots, and the air grows ever thicker with the stench of decrepitude.

Yet beneath this macabre veneer is an even more nightmarish truth. In the midst of this pit of monsters sits the Abhorrant Ghoul King upon a throne of mortal remains. Tall and powerful, everything about the king screams that he is a bestial predator, from his lithe, corded muscles to the dark hunger in his inhuman gaze. However, this is not how he appears to himself or his followers. They see him upon a gilt throne in a great hall. Next to him, his men-at-arms stand to attention or spar, ready for the call to war. Servants scurry about preparing another feast for their lord, or attend to the running of the kingdom. His thronging subjects are hale and hearty, well fed on the bounteous produce of his ordered lands. The yawning chasm between truth and perception is fuelled by a singular, all-consuming delusion, emanating from the twisted mind of the Ghoul King to infect every mordant in his presence. They believe themselves sane and civilised, and are incapable of seeing their own abject wretchedness.

Within the madness of a Flesh-eater Court, each individual has their role. The king is lord and master of all, an absolute monarch of a deranged nation. Sometimes, he might create other abhorrants to share in this glory, though they usually remain subservient to his desires. Those that do are known as sycophants, and can range from a single 'heir' to the throne to a whole brood of bloodsuckers taking on the roles and titles of the king's doting family. For example, in the first Flesh-eater Court established by the Carrion King, the Giblet Prince was the heir apparent and closest to his sovereign. The Offal Queen oversaw the bloodnurseries, caring for the newest of the brood, and making sure they fed regularly on the red bounty their father provided. Then there were the Sweetbread Princelings, chosen companions of the Giblet Prince, charged by the king to keep his heir safe, be it in the madness of battle or out on a hunt. Similar hierarchies exist in other courts, with some even sharing the names and titles of those first sycophants – these are the courts in which the Carrion King's delusion persists in its purest form.

Beyond the inner circle of a Ghoul King, favoured mordants see to the daily running of the court. Above all other mordants reign the Varghulf Courtiers, the greatest of which sometimes carries the ancient title of Marquis Gruelsop. Ferocious agents of the court, they lead the Royal Mordants, and are often trusted by their king with command of the court's armies. Crypt Infernal Courtiers and Crypt Haunter Courtiers are field commanders and earn titles like the Lord Marrowbroth or the Lord Liverbelch, overseeing the soldiers of the Deadwatch and the Abattoir respectively. The traditional position of Lord Chamberslough is held by a Crypt Haunter Courtier who rules over the Lickspittles keeping order at court. Then there are the monikers of Marquis Retchbile and Baron Gizzard, Crypt Ghast Courtiers who stand as marshals for the king's massed mordant armies, be it the stalwart and proud ranks of the King's Ghouls or the stealthy Ghoul Patrol.

Each Flesh-eater Court is a discrete kingdom, yet all swear allegiance to the Carrion King. In his absence, the mightiest of all abhorrants see his will fulfilled across the realms. These Abhorrant Archregents rule over vast empires comprising many separate courts, collecting flesh-tithes from the Ghoul Kings beneath them and delivering insane proclamations with the authority of their lord. Some allow their subservient Ghoul Kings to act autonomously in pursuing their gruesome agendas, insisting only that these lesser abhorrants provide their Archregent with worthy gifts. Others choose to oversee all matters within their empires, keeping close watch over their manifold holdings and a short leash on their petty Ghoul Kings. To a sane mind, a domain ruled by such an Archregent is like a continent-sized abattoir, with multiple courts working in unison to butcher and devour all who step inside their borders. In these nightmarish empires, the air itself seethes with madness.

Sycophants and mordants grovel before the throne of their sovereign, offering up grotesque gifts as a sign of fealty. The nightmarish sight is complemented by the reek of blood and offal, though in the eyes of the Flesh-eaters it is a stately affair in which each perfumed noble makes a grandiose display of their loyalty to the court.

# REVENANTS OF THE RAVAGED LANDS

**The Mortal Realms are host to many and varied Flesh-eater Courts. The greatest number reside in Shyish, for it was here that the Carrion King's insanity first took hold; but as subsequent generations of abhorrants spread further they found cannibals susceptible to madness scattered throughout the lands that had been ravaged by Chaos.**

## ENDLESS FEEDING GROUNDS

During the Age of Chaos, the realms suffered greatly. Bloodthirsty killers turned glittering continents into reeking charnel houses, and dark wizards loosed storms of sorcery that warped the landscape beyond recognition. In the wake of terrible wars, many lands became ripe for the slow, terrifying transformation into a Flesh-eater kingdom. Stumbling and shaking, the survivors of these fallen states emerged from the ruins of their once-great civilisations, only to face new and insidious threats. Starvation and madness took their toll, and the creatures turned to murder and cannibalism to survive. In time, packs of scavengers arose from among the survivors to prey upon their erstwhile kin, and the darkness beyond the campfires of marauding Chaos armies was filled with pale horrors and the sickening crunch and slurp of bones being devoured. To the abhorrants, the call of these hungry children was like a siren's song, and whether it took days, years or even centuries, a deranged ruler eventually arrived at each of these pits of despair and depravity to bring about a macabre transformation.

This sinister process still plays out in famished and forsaken territories across the Mortal Realms. In a dark mockery of the kingdom that came before, an abhorrant will swiftly set about creating, in his own delusional mind, a functioning state. Ragged pennants of flesh are hung above crumbling ruins. Scouting parties range out across the land, establishing fresh borders for their lord's armies to defend and seeking out plentiful hunting grounds with which to feed the populace. In the broken remains of cities, nests of ghouls take up residence, stockpiling food and weapons. These offal pits and midden heaps are the treasure houses of the court, and are closely guarded. More than one foe has battled their way bitterly through waves of frenzied Flesh-eaters expecting lost riches or precious grave goods, only to find craters filled with rotting meat and broken bones.

An Abhorrant Ghoul King is always ready for an attack against his lands. Whether he believes himself the master of a mighty fortress – which in reality is a crumbling castle long since abandoned by the conquerors that put it to the torch – or a nomad prince encamped for a time to secure supplies, he will ferociously protect what is his. Like knights of the realm, Crypt Flayers soar over the court's domain, drawn by the hissing cries of the Ghoul Patrol. These flying terrors shadow those who would defile their master's kingdom, while ghoul hosts lay cunning ambushes in the invader's path. United by their delusion, Flesh-eater armies show a level of coordination that is belied by their gruesome appearance, and that has been the doom of countless foes.

## THE MORTAL COIL

The other denizens of the Mortal Realms are only dimly aware of the madness afflicting the Flesh-eaters. In the eyes of most humans, aelves and duardin, they are grotesque and bestial creatures, driven by their insatiable hunger and utterly incapable of rational thought. The truth of their dark insanity is known only to those scholars who have deciphered the scrawls of mordants, and to those veterans who have faced the Flesh-eaters enough times in battle to recognise the focused intelligence that underpins their savagery.

In a similar fashion, when an abhorrant looks to the lands bordering his kingdom, he does not see the embattled nations and savage hordes that surround him for what they really are. In his mind's eye, these other mortals are twisted to fit his delusion, their appearance, words and motives mangled beyond recognition. Many a Freeguild caravan has passed through the desolate barrens of an abhorrant's kingdom, believing the ruin-scape to be devoid of life, only to be set upon by tearing claws and chomping teeth. To the Ghoul King and his mordants these interlopers appear as roving barbarian hordes, come to pilfer their granaries and abscond with their livestock. Similarly, the king's courtiers may be sent to butcher a nearby Arcanite Cult as it weaves profane sorceries and gives praise to Tzeentch, or to feast on the flesh of an ancient Slann attempting to conjure its saurus armies. But in the mind of the abhorrant he is simply sending the most learned nobles of his court to impart the spiritual wisdom of his kingdom to his parochial and somewhat backwards neighbours.

So warped in body and mind are the Flesh-eaters that most other mortals do what they can to avoid them entirely. The Idoneth Deepkin are particularly wary of them, for their memory magics have little effect on those so disconnected from reality. Amongst the Anvils of the Heldenhammer, certain Lord-Ordinators have used their scrying powers to glimpse the minds of abhorrants. They have seen the noble intent that lies behind so many of these creatures' actions, yet the enormities of the Ghoul Kings' deeds puts them beyond any hope of redemption.

## OUTPOURING OF MADNESS

As abhorrants spread their insanity across the Mortal Realms, their delusions manifested in different ways. To the untrained eye, the courts that have formed are equally depraved, yet the horrors endured by each nation of cannibals vary in their grotesqueness. Even in their basest state, a part of each wretch's mind clung to the glory of who their ancestors had once been – before the coming of Chaos and the ravages of war – and it was to these memories that the abhorrants anchored their insanity.

In Ulgu there had been vast networks of kingdoms for whom open war was anathema to their way of life. These shadow kingdoms fought each other with words and secrets, seeding spies amongst their rivals' retainers and using rumour and misdirection to support or undermine as they saw fit. Faced with the armies of the Dark Gods, these peoples were swiftly overrun, their extraordinary guile doing little to save them from the blade. Those who survived as cannibals clung to their culture of intrigue, and when swayed to the will of a mighty Archregent lost all memory that their whispering existence had ever been interrupted. The abhorrants that now rule these kingdoms send their courtiers to learn the heart of their rival or bend the ear of their ally, and the courtiers dutifully return to their sovereign bearing the mangled heart of an invading warlord or a severed head to be set at the foot of their Ghoul King's throne.

Throughout Ghyran there were nations of people who dwelt amongst the verdant forests. They ate only that which they grew in their hanging gardens, and made alliances with those alongside whom they lived, such as the Sylvaneth of Dreadwood Glade. When the armies of Nurgle invaded, blights and plagues ran rampant throughout the forest, and the peoples were forced to hunt down and eat those not yet afflicted or face starvation. This barbarity was unimaginable to the Ghyranites, so their minds were easily bent into believing that they still live a peaceful existence – they continue to think they are at one with nature, even as they hack and devour their former Sylvaneth allies.

These and countless other delusions exist throughout the realms, leading to vast kingdoms that are blind to their own atrocities. Though their once-glorious nations were brought to an apocalyptic end by the Age of Chaos, the Flesh-eaters believe that they held firm against the darkness, maintaining their values while the world around them went mad.

## NO REST FOR THE WICKED

The underworlds of Shyish are carved out of the collective belief of myriad mortals. A given culture's conception of the afterlife is formed from the raw amethyst magic of the Realm of Death, and it is to this land that the souls of that culture go upon their death. The mordants of the courts – despite their deathly pallor – are living creatures possessed of souls, and in the depths of their insanity still hold to the beliefs of their old culture regarding the afterlife.

So it was that when a new court was formed, the afterlife into which its mordants passed when they died remained largely unchanged. Courts who believed themselves to be pastoral fiefdoms had underworlds in which spirits dwelt amongst lush fields, spending days rearing herds of livestock and nights making merry with their fellow honoured dead. Similarly, mordants who saw themselves as gallant beastslayers spent their afterlife slaughtering endless series of monstrosities, holding aloft the severed heads as commoners showered them with flower petals. Many of these underworlds were reserved for those who lived pure and just lives, cleaving to chivalric codes and resisting temptation. Conversely, an afterlife of torment and penance awaited those who strayed from the path of honour. But in their deranged minds, mordants saw themselves as paragons of virtue, shielding the weak from evil while remaining untouched by corruption. This could not be further from the truth, yet their unshakable belief in the nobility of their actions ensured that, upon death, they pass blissfully into an underworld alongside the other souls of their decayed civilisation.

Since the Shyish necroquake, which saw a wave of unfettered death energy blasted across the Mortal Realms, the underworlds of the Flesh-eaters have undergone a marked change. Where once the souls of mordants passed into death as untainted souls, they have now begun carrying the horrifying reality of their existence with them into the afterlife. Upon parting with its body, a mordant's spirit no longer becomes a manifestation of the civilised being it believes itself to be. Instead it takes the form of a frenzied gheist that mercilessly cannibalises the other souls that share its underworld. In this way, the underworlds of the courts have become grim mirrors of their living kingdoms – nightmarish domains that are seen as paradise by their demented inhabitants. Vast regions of Shyish have succumbed to this insanity, and where once there were great swathes of peaceful Flesh-eater underworlds, there are now continent-spanning hellscapes through which hungering spectres prowl. Such is the force of the Flesh-eaters' delusion that dead mordants may not even notice their own incorporeality, and may rise en masse to fight alongside their still-living brethren.

# INDENTURED TO DEATH

**Nagash casts a dark shadow over the Realm of Death. The Great Necromancer claims all who toil under his gaze, including the mordants and their kings. Yet to the mordants Nagash is as much nemesis as he is deity, and for every ghoul who offers him fealty, another hates the God of Death with maddened fervour.**

Just as they are varied in the delusions they spread, abhorrants are divided in their view of the Great Necromancer. Some revere Nagash as a benevolent emperor and seek him out, hopeful of finding solace in his strength. Others loathe him as a force of destruction or dominance, forever fearful that Nagash is their doom or is seeking to cage them. Abhorrants either fawn at Nagash's feet or hide from his gaze in order to better pursue their own agendas. To all Flesh-eaters, however, Nagash's godhood is utterly undeniable.

From bone-thick feeding grounds, those courts allied to Nagash look up to crumbling statues of the Great Necromancer, offering their praise through mouthfuls of rotting meat. They do not see the grim and fleshless visage of a heartless god carved into the stone, but a divine face with piercing eyes, watching over the landscape with majestic authority. In the delusion of some abhorrant kings, Nagash appears as a beneficent deity wrapped in flowing golden robes, or wearing a shining crown as he smiles down from the sky. To honour their god, many courts have built shrines among the ruins of their kingdoms, such as the Corpsefane of the Nightlands, covered with ten thousand flayed faces, all stitched together with the same expression of rapture.

Those courts that hold Nagash in divine regard fight willingly in the armies of the dead. Mordants scuttle alongside clattering ranks of skeletal warriors and hordes of shambling deadwalkers, looking upon their allies as curiously uniformed soldiery from neighbouring kingdoms. Soulblight Vampires issue orders in a seductive tongue, but the magic-tinged words that compel the undead have little effect on the Flesh-eaters. Instead, the shared madness of the mordants leads them to hear only rousing speeches, stirring their hearts to new heights of bravery before they charge gallantly towards the foe. However, the deathless generals that command such combined armies do not look upon the Flesh-eaters with the same reverence. Vampires, Wight Kings and Necromancers respect the raw savagery of the mordants they lead, but are wary of the madness that infects their minds. Outside of the abhorrants themselves, no warlord could completely control such insanity.

Amongst the Flesh-eaters, the most fervent worshippers of Nagash see all other deities as pretenders. These courts march across the realms, tearing down graven images of false gods and slaughtering idolaters. The mordants of the Hollowmourne Grand Court are renowned for their zealotry in this regard, smashing the profane icons borne to battle by Chaos Lords, toppling the altars to Gorkamorka built up by greenskin tribes, and sacking cities in which statues to Sigmar have been erected. The bones of those slaughtered by the Hollowmourne mordants are then fused together into an effigy of the Great Necromancer, for in this way the newly conquered lands are deemed to be consecrated.

By contrast, those courts that distrust Nagash will travel as far away from the Realm of Death as possible in an attempt to escape the gaze of Nagash. Many of these courts would sooner face destruction or famine out in the wilds of the Mortal Realms than bow before him, and will go to great lengths to stay one step ahead of the God of Death. Some are forever on the move, like the Gluttonous Carnival. Its roving corpse caravans, heavy with scavenged meat, endlessly rumble across the land as they try to evade their imagined pursuers. Others construct vast fortresses, like the Witherclaw in Ghyran. Though its high walls exist only in its inhabitants' imaginations, its bone palisades and blood moats are real enough, and make it a formidable bastion that is fiercely defended against any suspected servant of Nagash sent to bring them to heel.

As much as their perceptions of Nagash differ, so too do the Flesh-eaters view the Great Necromancer's empire in Shyish through various lenses of madness. Some see the Shyish Nadir not as a plunging abyss in the heart of the realm, but as a soaring mountain atop which sits a paradisaic domain. To others, the yawning maw is the mouth of a great beast that they must ride out to slay, or a sacred prison in which Nagash himself is incarcerated.

Though every member of a Flesh-eater Court has been affected by the abhorrant's curse, and has therefore been instilled with madness born of death magic, mordants themselves are not dead. Their wretched existence can best be described as teetering on the edge of the grave – neither dead nor undead, but possessed of only the most grotesque semblance of life. As such, they are immune to the power Nagash wields over all dead things. With a whispered command, the Great Necromancer can order vast legions of skeletons and billowing armies of gheists to do his bidding, but his words have no hold on the lingering mortality of the mordants. Abhorrants, on the other hand, are vampires, and as such the call of Nagash resounds within the tattered remnants of their souls. However, the insanity carried by abhorrants gives them a certain degree of immunity from the Lord of Undeath, for though his will cannot directly be denied, his words are twisted beyond recognition in the warped minds of the Ghoul Kings and Archregents. In this way, it is the same curse that Nagash inflicted that keeps the descendants of the Carrion King from being controlled.

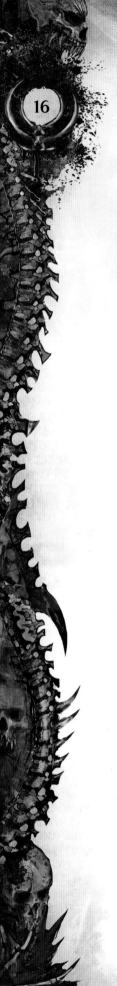

# THE COMING OF THE SOUL WARS

**The Flesh-eaters arose from the horrors of the Age of Chaos. Where other mortals races were brought to the brink of annihilation, the mordants grew steadily in number. But this time of expansion was not to last, for a storm was gathering in the heavens that threatened to wash away all the abhorrants had built.**

As the forces of the Dark Gods were approaching total domination over the Mortal Realms, Sigmar opened the Gates of Azyr and sent forth his Stormcast Eternals. Great forks of lightning lanced down across the realms and peals of thunder resounded throughout reality as the Stormhosts marched to battle. In a series of brutal campaigns, they wrested control of vital Realmgates from the servants of Chaos, allowing the scattered survivors of embattled civilisations to be united once more in defence of the realms. To the beleaguered humans, aelves and duardin, the Stormcast Eternals were an embodiment of hope, a manifestation of the God-King's implacable will sent to lead them out of their darkest hour. But to the Flesh-eaters, the sigmarite-clad warriors were something far more sinister.

The Stormcast Eternals drove back not only the Chaos-worshipping hordes, but all who opposed Sigmar's law. Greenskin tribes were hunted down and butchered, undead legions were shattered and sent back to their graves, and the kingdoms of the Flesh-eaters were besieged. Where the abhorrants had once reigned supreme, their madness spreading through ever-growing numbers of desperate wretches, they were now forced to defend their borders on multiple fronts – against the savagery of the Chaos warbands, and against the newly galvanised forces of Order. In the warped minds of the abhorrants and their subjects, the Stormcast Eternals were not noble warriors, but morbid abominations, wrought from dead flesh and imbued with unnatural life. The Flesh-eaters won many great victories over the Stormhosts, yet those foes they cut down were returned to life between battles, with the Stormcast Eternals who had been reforged multiple times appearing to the mordants as cadaverous monsters in increasing states of decrepitude.

## A TIME OF PORTENTS

Through long years of brutal conflict, the armies of Sigmar's pantheon clawed their way back from the point of obliteration. The servants of the Dark Gods still pursued their nightmarish campaigns across the Mortal Realms, and greenskin and ogor tribes continued to carve great swathes of devastation throughout the lands, but the dying embers of hope had been rekindled within many mortal peoples. As the endless wars raged on, and the number of slain rose ever higher, the realms were visited with new phenomena. Soothsayers, scryers, prophets and priests started to see deathly portents hinting at some great calamity that was soon to come. These visions were followed by physical manifestations – gheists burst from cracks in ancient tombs and the unquiet dead began clawing their way up from the grave in greater numbers than ever before. It quickly became apparent that this was the result of some dreadful power emanating from the heart of Shyish.

Nagash had watched as the denizens of the Mortal Realms fought and died. The soul of every living being was his by right, to be given over at the point of death, but no small number were being denied him, siphoned off by gods and sorcerers. Sigmar had stolen the souls of fearsome warriors to create his Stormcast Eternals, binding them to his service so that they would not pass into the underworlds when struck down, and through arcane rituals the aelves also kept the souls of their departed from passing to Nagash. Such affronts could not be borne, and so the Great Necromancer began gathering the realmstone of Shyish. From it he constructed an enormous inverted pyramid, towards which the death energy of the entire realm was drawn, before being blasted outwards in an apocalyptic eruption that rippled across existence.

## THE DEAD ARISE

In the wake of the Shyish necroquake, the souls of the dead pour from ancient crypts and mass graves across the Mortal Realms. But where Nagash planned to raise a Nighthaunt army beholden to his will, the death magic he unleashed was tainted by the touch of Chaos. Many of the risen gheists were twisted and misshapen, and instead of answering the Great Necromancer's call, they now roam wild, taking out their mindless torment on all in their path. This same corruption has augmented arcane energies across the realms in terrifying ways, birthing anarchic spells that never perish. Though Nagash's master stroke was soured, he has still brought about a time of dread – the Soul Wars – in which the followers of Sigmar, the armies of the Dark Gods and the greenskin hordes face an unending tide of death.

Amongst the courts, the spectral uprisings are seen as holy events. Each court filters the grim phenomena through the prism of their specific madness, but all believe that the unleashing of the underworlds into the other realms is a sign of a golden age of prosperity. In the vicinity of many courts, Nighthaunt processions tear across the lands, slaughtering the living with ghostly blades and incorporeal talons, and leaving naught in their wake but barren fields strewn with corpses. The Ghoul Kings see these processions as jovial communities of peasants, coming to harvest the crops that surround their kingdoms, and this delusion is given credence when every mordant is able to feast on the bounty that the Nighthaunts have provided.

To other courts, the teeming gheists are seen as learned ancestors and famed warriors returning to the mortal coil in the Flesh-eaters' hour of need. Mordants fight alongside thrashing Chainrasp hordes and whirling masses of Spirit Hosts against their common enemies, and in their madness the Flesh-eaters hear words of ancient wisdom and cries of encouragement in the wailing of the Nighthaunts.

Some courts have been overrun completely by the spectral processions, their feeding grounds now awash with unthinking gheists. In these places the Nighthaunts attack the Flesh-eaters with as much malice as they would any other living foe, perhaps remembering that their death came at the hands of these cannibals, or perhaps because it suits the will of Nagash. But even these courts believe themselves to be celebrating a time of prosperity. Where they battle against untamed spirits their madness has them participating in tournaments, and those Flesh-eaters that are slain are believed to have simply retired from the contest to drink and make merry with their new friends.

## SAINTS AND GODS

Of all the newly unleashed gheists, the most terrifying is Lady Olynder, Nagash's Mortarch of Grief. Calling out across the realms, she summons the anarchic Nighthaunt processions back to Shyish that they may be united as a single, unstoppable army. All mortals who gaze upon her are filled with soul-crushing woe, their every thought ripped from their mind and replaced with visions of sorrow – all, that is, except for the crazed Flesh-eaters. They see her not as a bringer of misery, but as a shining beacon of hope, a warrior saint who is the living embodiment of majesty. Instead of sobbing grief-stricken before her, many mordants and even abhorrants bow at her hem in respectful praise. More than one court has followed the processions of Lady Olynder to war, believing her to be a saviour sent by Nagash – or else the anointed champion of whatever gods their madness leads them to believe in – and they fight in her name with zealous fervour.

Some courts revere Nagash's other Mortarchs with similar ardour. Neferata, Mortarch of Blood, is a master seducer and manipulator, yet she is viewed as a peerless diplomat, travelling from empire to empire convincing tyrants and warlords to set aside their petty differences. Mannfred, Mortarch of Night, wages wars of cruelty and terror, but to some Flesh-eaters he is the noblest of generals, winning grand campaigns through compassion and unflinching civility. Arkhan, Mortarch of Sacrament, is the greatest of Nagash's students, second only to his master in his abilities with death magic, but to certain abhorrants and mordants is a beneficent scholar, seeking to spread his wisdom to the corners of the realms. Even to those courts who fear and despise Nagash, these Mortarchs may still be upheld as living saints. These Flesh-eaters do not see the Mortarchs as servants of Nagash, but as divine beings come to herald the return of the Carrion King.

*Flesh-eater Courts throughout the Mortal Realms see the Soul Wars as a time for celebration, parading across the lands waving banners and flags made from the flensed skins of their latest victims.*

# TALES OF MADNESS

Just as decay claims a mouldering corpse, the Flesh-eaters have spread out to infest the ruins of the Mortal Realms. Theirs are the deeds witnessed not by scholars and wise men, but by the desperate and hopeless, who either join their fiendish ranks or are devoured by courts of madmen.

## ● AGE OF MYTH ●

### THE FIRST DELUSION

Sigmar awakens from his slumber and begins travelling the Mortal Realms. Those primitive tribes he encounters are gifted with great wisdom and knowledge, and fledgling nations swiftly expand into sprawling civilisations. Amongst the peoples raised up by the God-King are whole kingdoms who proclaim this age of prosperity will never end. This mindset is passed down through the generations, and it is the descendants of these merry believers who will ultimately prove most susceptible to the abhorrants' curse.

### NOBILITY IN DEATH

The pantheon formed by Sigmar rules over the Mortal Realms, slaying the mighty godbeasts that roam the land and driving savage monstrosities beyond the borders of civilisation. Each god in the pantheon has many servants, and amongst those champions loyal to Nagash is a king known by countless names. A warrior, general and statesmen of great renown, this king travels far and wide, accompanied always by his court of noble knights. By his deeds Nagash gains worshippers in the furthest reaches of the Eight Realms.

### CRACKS IN SANITY

A growing shadow creeps over the lands as mortal nations examine their neighbours with jealousy, resentment and suspicion. Where once cooperation and community flourished, now the races of humans, duardin, aelves and orruks become increasingly factionalised, trusting only in their kindred, and sometimes not even that. But such animosity is not entirely natural – the Dark Gods look to the Mortal Realms from beyond the veil of reality, and through the hairline cracks in existence they exert their influence, stirring latent malevolent emotions to sudden fervour.

## THE SHROUDCAGE

Just as the Mortal Realms are beginning to devolve into anarchy, the bond between Nagash and his champion transforms into animosity. After being disfigured, Ushoran turns upon his master, using his knowledge of the Great Necromancer's empires to wage a devastating series of campaigns. Eventually, the Carrion King – as he comes to be known – is bested, and is imprisoned within the Shroudcage, there to rot in undying anguish.

## ● AGE OF CHAOS ●

### THE MADNESS OF THE CANNIBAL KING

After Nagash's betrayal of Sigmar during the opening stages of the Age of Chaos, the God-King rampages through Shyish, and in doing so topples the bastion that holds the Shroudcage. Ushoran escapes his prison and his madness begins to spread unchecked across the realms. Now utterly insane, the abhorrant's twisted view of the world manifests in various ways, with some of those afflicted by his delusion pledging themselves wholeheartedly to Nagash, while others swear oaths to lay low the Great Necromancer.

## NOBLE BEASTS

In Shyish, beastmen of the Slatehorns Greatfray roam the mountain range known as Betrayer's Barrier, slaughtering the dragons that roost in those peaks. Word of this reaches the abhorrants of the Morgaunt Grand Court – who believe the Shyishan dragons to be majestic gryphons – and together they amass their ghoul armies and march on the Barrier. After a long and gruelling campaign, the Slatehorns are eradicated, though not before they have slain the last of the dragons. Three of the Morgaunt Ghoul Kings pay their respects to the winged creatures, praying that they will continue to soar through the skies as magnificently in the afterlife. By some miracle, the creatures are resurrected, and henceforth serve as mounts for the Ghoul Kings.

### CLEANSED BY BLOOD

In their continual migrations, Flesh-eaters of the Hollowmourne Grand Court come across a horde of Bloodreavers indulging in a cannibalistic feast. The Flesh-eaters are repulsed by the sight, believing the Khornate savages to be knights from an infidel kingdom, gorging themselves on unclean meats. The mordants charge their foes, wiping them out to a man, then proceed to consecrate the battlefield by devouring the bodies of those they have slain, as well as the corpses that had been part of the Bloodreavers' feast.

### STAR-CROSSED

As the madness of the Flesh-eaters takes hold over more of the realms, the ancient Slann Starmaster Tesolesalak lays siege to the Dreamgheist courts in Hysh. But when Tesolesalak advances further into the Flesh-eaters' domain, he finds himself engaged on a battlefield that is surrounded by a score of Charnel Thrones. The raw insanity emanating from these grim constructs seeps across the battle lines, and before long even the Starmaster's inscrutable mind is being gnawed at by the Dreamgheists' delusion. As the battle rages on, the saurus and skink warriors conjured from Tesolesalak's mind become more and more deranged, appearing not as mighty soldiers, but as twisted monstrosities who attack their enemies and their allies with equal fervour.

## ☙ AGE OF SIGMAR ❧

### CLOUDED MINDS
The God-King Sigmar opens the Gates of Azyr and sends forth his Stormhosts, halting the Chaos advance on many fronts. Though bitter wars continue to rage, there is much rejoicing throughout the realms, for in the Stormcast Eternals do the beleaguered mortals see their salvation. But not so the Flesh-eaters – in their mangled minds they see only darkness in the gathering thunderheads, and to them the glistening ranks of sigmarite-clad warriors are but honourless cut-throats in the armies of a false god.

### BALANCE OF POWER
Deep in the Ghurish Gnarlwood, the abhorrant known as the Nightstalker sends his mordants to eradicate a tribe of Bonesplitter orruks. Since time immemorial, the Bonesplitterz have preyed on the gargantuan carnivores that prowl the ancient forest, but the Nightstalker sees them as lowly poachers, flouting his sovereignty by hunting in his royal grounds. Hundreds of ghouls descend upon the Bonesplitterz encampment, and in gruesome battle they tear the orruks limb from limb before feasting on the mangled green flesh. With their predators annihilated, the population of giant beasts within the Gnarlwood explodes, spilling out into the surrounding territories. The Astral Templars – already stretched to their limit against the Chaos hordes in the region – are forced to divert several Strike Chambers to contain the savage stampedes.

### WAGES OF DEATH
A Kharadron sky-fleet out of Barak-Urbaz is approached by a pallid envoy. He tells them that his king will pay fifty thousand gold coins to the mercenaries if they eradicate the Slaaneshi cults in the lands around his small kingdom. The Kharadron accept, and the last of the cultists are cut down by aethershot in a matter of weeks. When the duardin go to collect their payment, they are met not by a royal envoy, but by slavering ghouls, and in place of gold coins they are presented with thousands upon thousands of vertebral discs, each of which bears a scrawled image of the Carrion King.

### GOOD TIDINGS
Across the Mortal Realms, soothsayers and prognosticators foresee a time of great tribulation. Soon after, even those without mystic intuition are afflicted by grim dreams, or else come face to face with the growing numbers of risen dead. These portents cause terror to spread like plague, yet amongst the Flesh-eaters there is joy and celebration. In the clattering legions of skeleton warriors and moaning hordes of deadwalkers, the Flesh-eaters see hale and hearty peasants merrily returning to work the lands. Many Ghoul Kings proclaim that the coming harvests will be bountiful, and that these jocund times are to be celebrated with daily feasts.

### DARKNESS DESCENDS
In an attempt to establish a military way station, desert-dwelling Free Peoples construct the Dunekeep – a fortified outpost in the centre of the Reaver Wastes. Duardin masons build enormous walls around the outpost, which are then bound with aelven wards and lined with Ironweld artillery, making them more than capable of holding back the Khornate hordes and greenskin tribes of the region. For two decades the Dunekeep stands strong against marauding warbands, and the corpses of those repelled at its walls are left to bake in the harsh desert sun. Then, over a few short days, vast flocks of carrion birds begin circling above the fortress, their numbers so great they block out the sky. The defenders are shrouded in darkness and deafened by the shrill cawing, but this is only the prelude to the true horror that awaits them.

Hundreds of Crypt Flayers from the Blisterskin Grand Court descend through the clouds of vultures, swooping down to rip the Freeguild soldiers from the battlements before turning their attention on those stationed inside the outpost. Against this vertical assault, the Dunekeep's mighty walls only serve to pen in the terrified garrison.

### THE LUNATIC SEER
The Abhorrant Archregent known as the Skinless Sultan miraculously calculates where the Bad Moon will next appear. This feat draws the attention of Skragrott the Loonking, who wishes to add the abhorrant astronomer to his fungal asylum.

### AN HONOURLESS DEED
Following the Shyish necroquake, countless graves are opened throughout the Mortal Realms, allowing uncontrolled Nighthaunt processions to begin surging across the lands. A group of abhorrants from the Gristlegore Grand Court try to rein in one such procession, believing them to be frightened refugees in need of saving. The abhorrants block off a mountain pass in an attempt to corral and calm the howling gheists, but the Nighthaunts do not listen to the Flesh-eaters' offers of aid. Worse still, a mighty contingent from one of the Celestial Warbringers' Sacrosanct Chambers strikes down into the pass, banishing the trapped spectral horde and slaughtering the abhorrants. A single Ghoul King emerges alive, and he swears a vow of vengeance against the Stormcast Eternals for their barbaric and cowardly act.

### THE THRONE AWAITS
The confluence of death magic in the centre of Shyish plunges the city of Nagashizzar into a bottomless chasm from which nothing can escape. Those living souls not swallowed by the Shyish Nadir begin migrating further towards the edge of the Realm of Death. Many are never heard from again, and some return in a deranged state, babbling about a mighty ruler who shall come to be known across the lands. Each garbled account gives this figure a different name, but all give him the same title – the Carrion King.

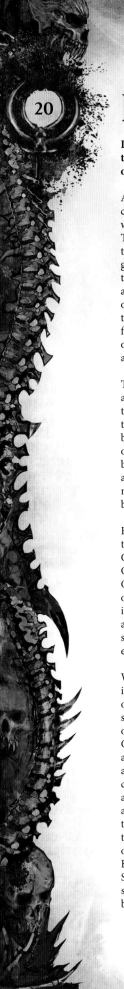

# DERANGED KINGDOMS

**Despite appearing like motley hordes, Flesh-eater armies display preternatural cunning and organisation on the battlefield. The blood-curdling snarls of abhorrants are heard by their mordant followers as crisply delivered orders, and through their shared madness the Flesh-eaters work to enact their gruesome stratagems.**

A Flesh-eater Court is a self-contained kingdom, at the heart of which sits an Abhorrant Ghoul King. These lords are the sinew that tethers the mordants together, bestowing grandiose delusions of nobility on their subjects. The king's mordant armies are completely in the thrall of their master, and at his command they scour the realms in search of fresh prey, their pale bodies pouring over the land like grave-worms over a decaying corpse.

There is usually but a single abhorrant king ruling a court, though in rare cases a council of the most powerful vampires might be in control instead – provided, of course, that they are united by a singular madness. Fledgling abhorrants whose delusions are not yet as powerful form the king's brood of sycophants and successors.

Beneath this 'royal family' stand the king's favoured lieutenants – Crypt Haunter Courtiers, Varghulf Courtiers and Crypt Infernal Courtiers, which serve as nobles of the court and lead its illustrious institutions. These are the largest and most dangerous of the king's servants, and they occupy the upper echelons of his kingdom.

When the entirety of the court is called to war, the Ghoul King often leads the army, but will sometimes give command to one of his sycophants or Varghulf Courtiers. Varghulfs drink long and deep from their master's veins, and so their connection with the court's sovereign is strong – they are entirely devoted to their liege, and for this reason are more trusted to enact his vision upon the Mortal Realms than any of the other courtiers. Like many Ghoul Kings, Varghulfs lead from the sky. Swooping over the battlefield, they screech at the warriors battling below them – a high-pitched sound

that is terrifying to their enemies but akin to the clarion call of a hunting horn to the soldiers of the king's court.

Other favoured courtiers may also be trusted to direct their own armies in battle, leading vanguard forces ahead of the main body of Flesh-eaters or raiding enemy settlements. When granted a position of command, a courtier speaks with the authority of their abhorrant sovereign, exuding the madness with which they have been so completely infused.

The bulk of the Flesh-eater population is formed of ghoul hosts that grow and shrink depending on the fortunes of their court. These are overseen by Crypt Ghast Courtiers, who to themselves and their troops are vaunted veterans possessed of the finest arms and armour. Individual regiments are led by Crypt Ghasts, all chosen from the most vicious and cunning of their kind. Ghast Courtiers often have grand and ancient titles, which they aspire to and treasure, even as they covet the attention of their king. Similarly, Crypt Ghasts strive to constantly prove their worth in battle, and with noble intentions drive themselves and the Crypt Ghouls they lead to ever-greater depths of depravity.

A single court may be roused to war by its Ghoul King to drive off an invading army or to defend his honour after a perceived slight. Courtiers and mordants are mustered and together they march to battle, scrabbling forwards with maws agape beneath banners of flapping skin. Such a campaign can reduce a well-fortified city to a slaughterhouse in a matter of days, but when an Archregent calls upon the courts under his command, the realms truly tremble. Hundreds of thousands of cannibal fiends tear across the lands, swallowing continents as they advance and drowning whole nations in gore.

Though each court has its own internal hierarchy, with noble titles and military ranks derived from the twisted depths of the Ghoul King's mind, many courts are arranged around similar principles. This structure is based upon that of the court founded by the Carrion King, and has been echoed countless times across the realms. This hierarchy is divided into three tiers, with the abhorrant sovereign at the top, surrounded by his sycophants and attendants at court. Below them are the elite soldiery of the Ghoul King's most trusted courtiers, who view themselves as knightly orders enacting the bidding of their liege. The lowest tier contains the vast might of the abhorrant's armies, his slavering Crypt Ghoul packs, serving as line infantry and scouting rangers. The majority of the courts that cleave to this hierarchy do so as a matter of tradition, believing they are maintaining the values of the greatest and most noble kingdom to have ever arisen within the Mortal Realms. But some abhorrants are so deluded that they believe themselves to be ruling over the First Court in the Carrion King's stead, going so far as to give their sycophants and courtiers the same names and titles as their ancient forebears.

## THE ABHORRANT GHOUL KING
*ABHORRANT*

The Abhorrant Ghoul King Greth the Decrepit rules over the Clatterbone Court in Shyish. As a close descendant of the First Court, the delusion that spreads from him to his followers aligns closely with that of the Carrion King.

### ROYAL FAMILY
Greth the Decrepit keeps his most trusted abhorrant subjects close at hand, to serve him in battle and to join him in feasting.

**SYCOPHANTS**
*ABHORRANTS*

### ATTENDANTS AT COURT
The obsequious Lord Chamberslough fawns over the king and fights with horrific vigour.

**LORD CHAMBERSLOUGH**
*CRYPT HAUNTER COURTIER*

**LICKSPITTLES**
*CRYPT HORRORS*

### DEADWATCH
Lord Marrowbroth commands the defence of Greth's kingdom.

**LORD MARROWBROTH**
*CRYPT INFERNAL COURTIER*

**CURSPOCK**
*CRYPT FLAYERS*

**VILESCRAPE**
*CRYPT FLAYERS*

**SLOPCRAW**
*CRYPT FLAYERS*

### ABATTOIR
Lord Liverbelch is charged with keeping the king's stores stocked with fresh flesh.

**LORD LIVERBELCH**
*CRYPT HAUNTER COURTIER*

**HARFLECK BUTCHERS**
*CRYPT HORRORS*

**DRUBSCROTE SLAUGHTERERS**
*CRYPT HORRORS*

**BOGLEECH BOTTLEWASHERS**
*CRYPT GHOULS*

### ROYAL MORDANTS
Marquis Gruelsop is a savage commander and Greth's most trusted courtier.

**MARQUIS GRUELSOP**
*VARGHULF COURTIER*

**GLUGRASP**
*CRYPT HORRORS*

**SPLEENLICK**
*CRYPT FLAYERS*

**SLUGSOUR**
*CRYPT GHOULS*

### GHOUL PATROL
Baron Gizzard and his ghouls stalk the wastelands at the edge of the court's domain.

**BARON GIZZARD**
*CRYPT GHAST COURTIER*

**ILLCREEP**
*CRYPT GHOULS*

**SLUMCRAWL**
*CRYPT GHOULS*

**FILCHLURK**
*CRYPT GHOULS*

### KING'S GHOULS
When new prey has been found, it is Marquis Retchbile who leads the charge into battle.

**MARQUIS RETCHBILE**
*CRYPT GHAST COURTIER*

**GLUGSPEW**
*CRYPT HORRORS*

**SPLEENSCAB**
*CRYPT GHOULS*

**SLUGSPOIL**
*CRYPT GHOULS*

### ROYAL MENAGERIE
*TERRORGHEISTS AND ZOMBIE DRAGONS*

Many and varied are the delusions of the abhorrant kings, and their courts are just as diverse. Shown here is an example of the structure of a court and its titled courtiers, but every court has its own peculiarities and may have a structure that only loosely resembles this.

# DARK LEGACIES

The military formations of the Flesh-eaters harken back to the First Court in Shyish. Various abhorrants have adopted elements of this twisted structure into their delusions, even believing their own sycophants and generals to be the same that long ago served the Carrion King.

## CARRION KING
### SOVEREIGN OF THE COURT

Every abhorrant is an heir to the Carrion King, who was first to bear the curse of insanity. The delusions of a court's princes and lords are splinters of his original madness, warped echoes of the noble customs and practices of the warriors who pledged themselves to the Carrion King so long ago. The regal names they bore were twisted by the march of years to become vile parodies of the once-great men and women they represent.

## SYCOPHANTS
### THE ROYAL FAMILY

The sycophants are the memory of the Carrion King's ancient family given form. Names like the Offal Queen and Giblet Prince hold a shred of the Carrion King's history, and in some stories, they become the Awful Queen and Gibbeted Prince, hinting at the fate that befell them.

## LORD CHAMBERSLOUGH
### VIZIER OF THE ATTENDANTS AT COURT

It is said the Lord Chamberslough once vied for control of the Carrion King's domains, yet his worth as a commander was such that he was taken in by the Carrion King, becoming a loyal servant and Vizier of the Attendants at Court.

## LORD MARROWBROTH
### FIRST KNIGHT OF THE DEADWATCH

Pride radiates from the Lord Marrowbroth, for he is the champion protector of the king. He was the most loyal of the Carrion King's servants, the Lord of the Harrow Wrath armies that defended the kingdom from Nagash's Mortarchs.

## LORD LIVERBELCH
### MASTER OF THE ABATTOIR

The Lord Liverbelch is the master of banquets and chief taster to the king. Whole regions of the Carrion King's empire were harvested for his blood feasts, and the Lord Liverbelch gathered fair-skinned youths from faraway kingdoms to quench the thirst of his sovereign.

## MARQUIS GRUELSOP
### COMMANDER OF THE ROYAL MORDANTS

Loyal to a fault, the Marquis Gruelsop stands as the greatest of the king's courtiers and leader of the Royal Mordants. The marquis turned the slaves and prisoners that are his wards into some of the finest soldiers in the king's army.

## BARON GIZZARD
### CHIEF RANGER OF THE GHOUL PATROL

A keen-eyed hunter, the Baron Gizzard leads the king's scouts. Stories say the original baron was once a commoner who patrolled the icy Helfrost Empires at the kingdom's edge, though he became a favoured servant of the king.

## MARQUIS RETCHBILE
### LORD OF THE KING'S GHOULS

Martial might is the domain of the Marquis Retchbile. While Ushoran was served by many skilled generals, the marquis is the memory of these warriors confused into a single figurehead by the madness passed down by the Carrion King.

## THE ROYAL MENAGERIE

The Carrion King kept many pets from his journeys across Shyish and the realms beyond. Favoured among his mounts were the Blood Drakes and Chiropteran Behemoths. Though the names and deeds of these beasts have long been lost to history, each abhorrant king fondly remembers these creatures and lavishes his attention on the Zombie Dragons and Terrorgheists of his menageries, as if the huge undead creatures were his own living offspring.

# MORGAUNT GRAND COURT

**From the Prime Innerlands of Shyish come the heaving masses of the Morgaunt Grand Court. Countless pallid bodies stained by their latest slaughter surge across the desolate landscape to sunder all in their path. Theirs are amongst the oldest courts in all the realms, and in them the Carrion King's madness remains at its purest.**

The courts that make up the Morgaunt Grand Court are the descendants of living kingdoms in the Realm of Death. Their culture had been one of chivalry and honour, in which the gallant and strong fought to protect the weak and unfortunate. When the peoples in these kingdoms were beset by invaders or plagued by prowling monstrosities, the kings would gather knights and soldiers to their banners and march out to purge their lands of wickedness. It was said that to become a member of a king's court in those days, an aspiring knight had to prove his bravery and selflessness through service to the king's subjects. A knight might have laid low a shambling cadaver titan that was feeding on the people of a particular village, or hunted down the draco-vulture that had been gorging itself on livestock in a given region and plunged his blade through the winged beast's black heart. Similarly, to serve in a sovereign's army a soldier had to uphold the core tenets of chivalry, and had to be willing to lay down his life for the least of the king's subjects.

These kingdoms prospered in the Age of Myth, their influence extending from the Amethyst Princedoms in the north to the Glittering Marsh in the south. They were hailed by their allies as exemplars of civilisation, and respected by the few enemies they had as worthy and honourable foes. They also lived in peace with the dead within their borders, treating the spirits of the departed with the same dignity as they did the living – and it was this coexistence with their ancestors that caused these kingdoms to side with Nagash when Shyish was beset by invaders. The armies of Sigmar and Chaos tore through the Realm of Death, sundering the magnificence of the chivalric civilisations, scattering their peoples, and driving them to the brink of annihilation.

Yet from the crumbling ruins the Morgaunt Grand Court arose. Gifted with the madness of the Carrion King, the mordants saw their corpse-strewn homelands as lush and verdant once more, and their slavering abhorrants as pinnacles of nobility. They set about reclaiming their territories from the invaders, driven by the belief that they could return their lands to a state of peace. But in truth, the rise of these courts only served to further soak the northern reaches of the Prime Innerlands with gore. Wherever abhorrants and courtiers travelled, ghouls flocked to their side in droves – the bonds of loyalty between high-born and commoners having persisted across generations of cannibalistic savagery – and together they set about slaughtering all who trespassed within their domain.

Since the Age of Chaos, Morgaunt abhorrants have spread throughout the realms, drawing mordants to their side in overwhelming numbers wherever they establish new courts. They see other living beings as invading armies or rampaging monstrosities, and so march out en masse to cleanse their lands. They look to Nagash as their patron god, and see all who oppose him as wicked and ignoble. Above all else, they have a fierce loathing of Sigmar. The Morgaunt courts believe that, were it not for the God-King's betrayal, Nagash would have been able to repel the forces of Chaos from Shyish once and for all.

*Amidst the bones, skin and dripping viscera, ancient symbols of the Morgaunt Grand Court can be seen daubed in blood.*

# HOLLOWMOURNE GRAND COURT

**Packs of hulking cannibals stampede towards their foe to the sound of insane snarling. As the armies of the Hollowmourne Grand Court close in, Crypt Horrors charging at the fore launch themselves into the opposing lines, obliterating shield walls and butchering the enemy's ordered ranks.**

More so than any other Flesh-eaters, the history of the Hollowmourne Grand Court is shrouded in mystery. In a long-dead age, the empire that spawned the Hollowmourne courts extended across the Mortal Realms. Its glorious emperor – whose name has been lost to the ravages of time – brought knowledge and civilisation to those whom he encountered, fostering harmony between disparate lands and prosperity for all. In his travels throughout the realms, he discovered many wondrous relics, some of which he used to help lift up his people, and others that he deemed too dangerous for mortal use. In order to protect those in his empire, this emperor secreted the arcane implements and eldritch devices he had found within enchanted vaults, and in this way kept them hidden until a time in which they would be needed. Among the few who had knowledge of these vaults was an order of royal families from Chamon known as the Knights of the Hollowmourne, who knew not what was in the vaults, only that they must be protected at all costs.

When the servants of the Dark Gods began to sweep across the Mortal Realms, the Knights of the Hollowmourne were sent to secure the vaults against the taint of Chaos. Every kingdom dedicated to the order rode swift into hostile territory, their knights clad in the finest armours of Chamon. As they advanced they swore oaths that their duty would not go unfulfilled, but their enemies were too powerful, and their defiant crusade was shattered. The tattered remnants of the order kept moving, trying to outpace the enemy. When rations ran out, the peasants were eaten next, for the knights could not give up their horses if they hoped to ever fulfil their duty. But eventually, even the steeds were consumed, and it was this most unthinkable act that opened the minds of the Hollowmourne to madness.

The Hollowmourne Grand Court is all that remains of this once-proud crusade. While they still believe themselves to be a noble order of royal knights, heavily armoured horsemen towering above their enemies on the battlefield, in truth their bodies have grown to monstrous proportions after generations of gorging upon flesh. In battle, the largest of their number barrel ahead of the throng, charging out like lancers to shatter the enemy's defences, leaving those mordant packs that follow to feast upon the broken bodies of the dead and dying. Long gone are the resplendent suits of mail that once defined this order, its last vestige the oxidised colouration of the mordants' sickly flesh.

The Hollowmourne courts continue to search for the buried relics they were sent to defend, their abhorrants regularly launching new crusades into enemy lands. After annihilating the foe on the open field, the Flesh-eaters slaughter their way through towns and strongholds alike with terrifying speed, digging up tombs and graveyards in the blind hope that they will find what they are seeking. Usually such frenetic searches yield only rotting corpses, though in their delusion the Flesh-eaters see these as sacred artefacts deposited by their dimly remembered emperor. The largest of the Hollowmourne greedily devour these corpses, secure in the belief that they are keeping precious relics they have discovered from the clutches of the enemy.

*This coat of arms is a grim mockery of the crossed blades of the Knights of the Hollowmourne, which symbolised their oath to their emperor.*

# BLISTERSKIN GRAND COURT

**Darkness envelops the battlefield as the mordants of the Blisterskin Grand Court fill the sky. The flapping of leathery wings and the screeching of hundreds of hungering mouths deafens those below, drowning out all thoughts of hope and heralding the gruesome slaughter that is to come.**

The Flesh-eaters of the Blisterskin Grand Court are instantly recognisable by the hideous burns that cover their bodies. Long and wretched lives spent terrorising the sun-blasted plains of Aqshy have left these creatures with gaping patches of peeled skin, beneath which layers of charred musculature and bleached bone lie exposed. As they scrabble across deserts and barren lands in search of fresh victims, the reek of seared meat precedes their advance. But even if their prey catches wind of this acrid scent there is little chance of escape, for the armies of the Blisterskin Grand Court move at terrifying speed, following the lead of winged mordants and courtiers as they encircle their enemies.

The empire from which the Blisterskin courts arose was founded upon various forms of sun worship. Their priesthood was made up of members of multiple royal families, with kings and queens of neighbouring city states leading their people in sacred rites. During the harvest season, a third of every crop was given up as sacrifice – sheaves were placed atop the tallest ziggurats and left to be claimed by the sun, thereby ensuring that the next harvest would be abundant. At high noon, royals and commoners alike retreated indoors while the sun was at its most intense, an act of humble acknowledgement of its wrathful glory. Though these kingdoms were dotted across Aqshy, they knew the light of the sun emanated from Hysh, and they saw this distant realm as the sacred place from which all illumination and wisdom pour into existence. They actively sought out other civilisations to whom they could spread their culture, proselytising such nations as Bataar, Aspiria, and the Agloraxi in the west of Aridian. With these states they shared their most sacred beliefs, imploring all to honour the sun so that darkness might never fall across the lands.

When the armies of Chaos swept across Aqshy, the sun-worshippers were driven from their homes, their cities and crops set ablaze. With no harvests to sacrifice, they gave over the weak and old as burnt offerings, and prayed desperately for the sun to scour the legions of the Dark Gods from the realm. Their descent into wretchedness was swift and irreversible, yet the hope of the scattered survivors was rekindled by the arrival of mighty abhorrants. Afflicted by madness, the sun-worshippers believed they had finally gained the enlightenment they had always sought. No longer did they humble themselves by hiding from the sun, instead choosing to bask in its full fury, their flesh cooking in the blazing heat. The most pious amongst them were blessed with wings with which to rise ever closer to the sun, while the rest looked upon them with awe, following their swift flights with zealous fervour.

The Blisterskin Grand Court continues to send its members to its neighbours' lands, but where once they spread tenets of devotion, they now sow only horror across Aqshy and beyond. The royalty still guide their subjects in acts of worship, ensuring that offerings are given up after each harvest. As such, when the armies of the Blisterskin courts descend upon their enemies, a third of those they slaughter are left to fry in the sun, leaving great swathes of blackened and bloated corpses that tell of the Flesh-eaters' presence.

*The motifs of the Blisterskin Grand Court depicted the common folk and the royalty all looking upwards towards the glorious light of the sun.*

# GRISTLEGORE GRAND COURT

**Where once they lived in harmony with the lands around them, the Gristlegore courts now rampage across Ghur, butchering all they see. They believe themselves to be ruled by tranquil and peace-loving kings, but the grim truth is that the abhorrants of these courts are beings of pure frenzy.**

The crack of boulders being smashed aside and trees being uprooted precedes the advance of the Gristlegore Grand Court. Those they are hunting huddle together in defensive positions, listening as the insane snarling of the Flesh-eaters draws ever closer. Monstrous howls rise above the din as abhorrants, courtiers and great winged beasts burst through the dense foliage, and with savage haste tear their startled enemies to bloody ribbons.

The armies of the Gristlegore Grand Court are led by champions of peerless ferocity. Fighting with gruesome fervour, these warriors hack down multiple foes with every passing heartbeat and launch waves of amethyst magic that pulverise whole ranks of the enemy. Only the undead creatures of the Ghoul Kings' menagerie have any hope of keeping pace with the rampant butchery.

The ferocity of the Gristlegore courts is in stark contrast to the culture of the Tranquil Kingdoms from which they arose. Before succumbing to the abhorrant's curse, the people of this Ghurish civilisation found ways to live in balance with their savage surroundings. Slavering beasts, carnivorous plants and predatory mountains were all viewed with the greatest respect, and were treated as sovereign beings. The highest virtues were introspection and contemplation, whereas hunting and killing were seen as necessary evils to be avoided when possible. Though the realm in which they lived abounded with predators, the people of the Tranquil Kingdoms sought peace where they could find it, spending long weeks fasting and meditating. When forced to war, the nobility rode at the fore to engage the enemy first, for by risking their own lives they hoped to spare their subjects from the horrors of open battle. These nobles honed the arts of swordplay and spellcraft to perfection, and were able to best many opponents at once – but their skill could not save them from the coming of Chaos.

As the armies of the Dark Gods stormed through Ghur, the Tranquil Kingdoms descended into anarchy. Peaceful minds were filled with panic, and the common folk called upon their lords to face the coming hordes. But though they fought valiantly the nobility could not save their people, and were forced to watch as their subjects were put to the blade and their cities razed to the ground. With no one left to fight for, these disgraced royals wandered aimlessly, until they were found by powerful abhorrants and once more given purpose.

Now transformed by their insanity, the royals of the Gristlegore Grand Court prowl the realms like packs of alpha predators. In their minds they still seek balance and harmony, even as they shred their prey to gruesome chunks. Their desire to be at one with their surroundings causes them to pierce their own flesh with shards of Ghurish realmstone, and they believe they are purifying themselves through fasting even when dripping hunks of meat are lodged in their maws. To the Gristlegore abhorrants, every strike or arcane manifestation is measured, delivered with precision only after all other paths to victory have been contemplated – yet to see such a beast in action is to behold a mindless, thrashing monstrosity.

*Only the savage royalty of the Gristlegore Grand Court are depicted in their heraldry, for to them falls the responsibility of protecting their people.*

# ABHORRANTS

In contrast to the regal kings and emperors they see themselves as, abhorrants are truly monstrous beings. They are the vampiric heirs of the Carrion King, capable of slaughtering their way through entire enemy armies, and it is through them that his curse is spread across the Mortal Realms.

## ARCHREGENTS

The longer that a Ghoul King exists in its state of madness, the more powerful it becomes. Some believe that this is simply the curse of Ushoran replicating belligerently in the vampire's clotted veins. Others have suggested that it is the strength of the abhorrant's own insanity that bolsters the will and martial might of the creature. As the centuries creep by, the abhorrant becomes ever more corded with iron-hard muscle, its hide ever thicker and more leathery. The vampire's madness deepens, its conviction in its own supremacy reaching such fanatical levels that it leaves traces of its crazed visions superimposed upon reality. Not only do the abhorrant's courtiers become ever more dedicated and loyal to their master, but even those who battle the Flesh-eaters begin to perceive flashes of the abhorrant's delusions, flickering like half-seen flames about the edges of their vision. In time, this insanity extends beyond the borders of a single kingdom, binding mordants and other abhorrants into a united empire.

Each Abhorrant Archregent rules over the Ghoul Kings within its domain. Where a Ghoul King requires the aid of its courtiers to rally the masses and command its armies into battle, an Archregent has such far-reaching and indomitable will that it can achieve this feat all by itself. Some amongst the Flesh-eaters believe them to be mouthpieces of Ushoran, and certain Archregents even claim to have attended the court of the Carrion King.

Where Abhorrant Ghoul Kings are ferocious hunters that lead their armies from the fore, Archregents become brooding and reclusive. Though it possesses the raw strength to punch through a castle gate, or tear an armoured knight of Chaos in two with its bare talons, it takes a great deal for an Abhorrant Archregent to bestir itself to action. While it prowls its innermost sanctums, the running of its empire is left to petty Ghoul Kings, who maintain the flesh harvests and carouse at the head of bloody feasts in the Archregent's honour.

Only when a truly mighty threat to the kingdom arises does an Abhorrant Archregent take to the battlefield, and then it is a force to behold. Sprinting as fast as the wind, the Archregent tears through its enemies as though they were wet parchment. Blood flows in rivers as the ancient abhorrant slakes its deranged thirst, before summoning its elite warriors to its side and charging forwards to slaughter those foes that remain.

## GHOUL KINGS

An abhorrant king is the vicious ruler of a Flesh-eater Court. Whether scrambling across the ground with terrifying speed or riding upon the back of an undead monstrosity, an Abhorrant Ghoul King is a savage embodiment of insanity. Time and the curse of the Carrion King have given the abhorrants a hideous appearance, far removed from the ageless beauty of other vampires. However, they are just as deadly as any of their bloodsucking kind. This is most evident when the abhorrant rapaciously feeds on still-living enemies, streams of gore spilling down its face as he drains the vital essence from organs and hunks of flesh that it rips from his foes.

If the size and supernatural strength of an abhorrant king were not enough to strike fear into its foes, then there is also the madness that burns in its eyes. The vampire's delusion makes it a terrifying and unpredictable opponent, much feared by the races of the Mortal Realms. Ghoul Kings lead from the fore, surging towards the foe alongside their most favoured courtiers with packs of slavering mordants scrabbling behind them to join in the slaughter. Upon reaching the enemy lines, the abhorrant carves a brutal path through all before it, severing heads and limbs with each swipe, ripping bones and organs from still-living bodies before devouring the dripping offal. Whole swathes of soldiers are cut down by the Ghoul King's brutality, yet the true targets of its fury are the generals who have lead trespassers into its sovereign domain. Driven by the belief that it is a just noble, and that almost all creatures outside its court are savage barbarians, the king offers no quarter to threats against its people. Perhaps more frightening than the conviction this madness lends the king is its infectious nature. Those who linger too long in the abhorrant's presence risk losing their own minds, until they too see the king as it sees itself – a radiant and sovereign ruler with unquestioned authority.

Abhorrants, like many vampiric creatures, are powerful wizards, steeped in the magic of death and darkness. Abhorrant Ghoul Kings can use their fell wizardry to knit together their wounds, mend the broken bodies of their mounts, hurl sorcerous bolts or even summon troops with but a gesture. In their deranged minds, they believe themselves to be conduits of holy power or benevolent practitioners of magic. A Ghoul King may speak an ensorcelled command for its enemies to kneel before it, and to its eyes they immediately drop to the floor in humble acquiescence – but in truth its words summon tendrils of necrotic energy that rip the limbs from its foes, leaving only the mutilated torsos to writhe pathetically in the mud. The abhorrant can also amplify the madness of its followers, causing their insanity to manifest physically. Mordants are made to believe they are wearing suits of impenetrable armour, and the sheer strength of their magically fuelled delusion causes swords and spears to bounce harmlessly from their flesh. Others see themselves wielding ensorcelled weapons that strike and parry with arcane alacrity, when in reality the Ghoul King's magic sends the mordants themselves into a fury in which they thrash at their foes with unnatural speed and savagery.

It is via the same dark wizardry that the abhorrant is able to transform a wretched cannibal into a mordant – it is the vital ingredient in his sordid feasts, and the key to expanding his court. With a delicate stir of one of its claws, it can imbue blood draughts with bizarre power, transforming all who sup upon them into disturbing horrors slaved to its will.

## CHARNEL THRONES

Grim constructions rise above the bloodstained wastelands and reeking piles of carrion flesh that mark an abhorrant's domain. Built upon the ruins of once-grand castles and wrought from corpse-matter, these Charnel Thrones are the nightmarish seats of power from which the Archregents and Ghoul Kings rule over their subjects. Upon such a throne, an abhorrant sees itself seated on a work of artistry without parallel. The ancient bones that form the struts and spars of the throne are perceived as glittering rods of gold and silver, while gouged claw marks and remnant pieces of sinew are believed to be ornate filigree and inlaid gemstones.

As the ravenous packs of a court spread further into the surrounding lands, their sovereign orders ever more Charnel Thrones to be constructed. An abhorrant's master masons – the courtiers and sycophants to whom it imparts visions of its desired construction – are given the task of gathering materials and building a new throne. These masons scavenge battlefields and graveyards, seeking out skeletal pieces to be used in fulfilling the grand design. Only the bones of those who have been killed by an abhorrant's deranged death magic are fit for this purpose. Thousands of remains are picked through to find those in which the arcane energies of Shyish have soaked down to the marrow, with those found unworthy being cast aside as scrap.

When the Charnel Throne is at last pieced together, and the abhorrant perches itself upon it for the first time, the bones begin to scream and shake under the unbearable weight of its madness. From that point on, the throne is a conduit for the abhorrant's delusion, casting its insanity into the mind of all who behold it. The hideous wailing and ceaseless clatter of a Charnel Throne is enough to drive the enemies of the Flesh-eaters insane, and the morbid din echoes across the landscape for leagues in every direction, drawing distant packs of mordants to come bow before their king.

# COURTIERS

**Misshapen monsters, the Flesh-eater courtiers stand as hunchbacked lords within an abhorrant king's court. Grown strong upon the tainted blood of their master, these mordant leaders wade into battle, directing the king's armies as their lesser kin cluster in deranged adoration around their clawed feet.**

## VARGHULF COURTIERS

Favoured servants of the king, Varghulf Courtiers hold the highest rank a mordant can earn. They are the most trusted members of the court, and the most likely to lead an army if their monarch is otherwise occupied. Even when flying to battle alongside its sovereign, a Varghulf acts as a monstrous marshal, its howls carrying far to draw more Flesh-eaters into the combat. It is to these beasts that leadership over the hand-picked Royal Mordants falls, with some Varghulf Courtiers even being dubbed Marquis Gruelsop, the same title as that given by the Carrion King.

As befits their position, Varghulfs are gore-drenched monsters in combat, their fury only being surpassed by Abhorrant Archregents and Ghoul Kings. When surrounded by enemies, a Varghulf enters a terrifying frenzy, slaughtering faster than the eye can follow. Varghulfs are possessed of a voracious hunger, and as they tear a red road through a battle they rip great chunks off their prey, which they cram down their gullets then and there. Packs of smaller mordants scurry in their wake, doing their best to keep up with the blinding pace of the Varghulf's slaughter and snatching up any discarded pieces of meat

that fall from its maw. As Varghulfs consume their prey they are swiftly reinvigorated, muscles reknitting and rents in their flesh closing up in moments – and it is not only flesh that they feed upon. With lolling tongues they lap up dark energies from the air, devouring the sorcerous tendrils that erupt when abhorrants use their insane magic to cast spells or summon the dead. This foul energy strengthens such a beast, giving it might beyond even that suggested by its massive frame.

## CRYPT HAUNTER COURTIERS

Creatures of rotting flesh and twisted bone, the Crypt Haunter Courtiers are among the strongest of an abhorrant's mordant servants. They have supped from the Ghoul King's veins, and his dark magic has transformed them. Most mordants given a pure draught of the king's blood devolve so far into savage insanity that they end up tearing themselves apart in a frenzy of self-loathing, but those who survive are reborn with monstrous strength. In battle, they are brutal fighters who lead from the front, bathing in the rain of viscera caused by their ferocious attacks. Crypt Horrors respond unquestioningly to the orders of these courtiers, in their madness seeing them as fearless commanders clad in gleaming armour.

Crypt Haunter Courtiers are trusted members of the court who hold high status, and are respected and feared by all who serve the king. They also enjoy rare autonomy amongst their mordant kin, and those that are granted the rank of Lord Liverbelch will be despatched at the head of an Abattoir of ghouls and horrors, leading the scrabbling packs from the front lines. When they return victorious, it is also their duty to prepare the royal feast, and test the dishes to be set before the king.

## CRYPT GHAST COURTIERS

The Crypt Ghast Courtiers are vile creatures gifted in the ways of war. Displaying a measure of intelligence beyond that of their fellow cannibals, these crook-back champions are frenzied field commanders for the Abhorrant Ghoul Kings' armies. Forever jockeying for position, their first priority is to fawn before their sovereign and present him with gifts of freshly torn flesh. On the most servile Ghast Courtiers the Ghoul King bestows various titles to denote their status, sometimes gifting them with splintered shards of bone or other gruesome fetishes as medals for worthy service. In their minds, Crypt Ghasts are the noble heroes of the realm, clad in shining armour, with pennants snapping on the ends of their weapons. So armed with delusion, they proudly lead the court's troops to war, sniffing out tasty prey either at the head of endless ranks of foot soldiers or ranging ahead with scouting parties.

Like all mordants, Crypt Ghast Courtiers have been corrupted by their king's madness. Most were once great heroes, wizards or sages who fell into despair and cannibalism. Some even commanded armies in brutal campaigns fought against the Flesh-eaters, before defeat and then anguish transformed them into the very creatures they had sought to eradicate. Though wretched, they retain shreds of what they once were, and they enforce their peculiarities upon the ghouls they lead. If a particular Ghast Courtier was given to gluttony in their former life, the mordants that serve under them will partake in staggering displays of gorging, creating a grim simulacrum of the fine feasts their leader once enjoyed. If the Ghast Courtier was cruel, their followers exact as much pain as possible from the foe, often flensing and carving their enemies' bodies long after the point of death. If they were cunning, their soldiers melt from the very shadows in the wake of their nefarious master. A king will choose a Crypt Ghast Courtier's role based upon the creature's talents and inclinations, utilising them against the many enemies of the court.

## CRYPT INFERNAL COURTIERS

Crypt Infernal Courtiers are created when a Crypt Flayer has performed a heroic deed that the king deems worthy of reward. A banquet is held where individuals so honoured are fed the flesh of an undead dragon. Their guts mutate agonisingly, allowing these predators of the sky to exhale lethal clouds of noxious fumes, much like the beast they have eaten. These flying courtiers lead the Deadwatch, the Abhorrant Ghoul King's personal bodyguard. Gifted with exceptional senses, they can detect enemies from leagues away, identifying their victims by scent alone, and swooping off into the night to bring back gory prizes for their dark master.

When an Abhorrant Ghoul King rides to war astride his Terrorgheist or Zombie Dragon, Crypt Infernal Courtiers often soar at his side, vying for their lord's attention. Screaming summons to their kin, the courtiers lead daring strikes against the most formidable foes, rising high above the battlefield before folding their wings and plunging into the heart of the enemy lines. When they emerge from combat, their mouths are dripping with gore and the juices of burst organs, and their talons are covered with chunks of flesh and shattered pieces of bone. Only those most doughty of foes can survive being skewered by the Infernal Courtier's hooked claws, yet these victims are simply carried back to the Abhorrant Ghoul King, presented to him as prisoners. In his madness, the Ghoul King may order an Infernal Courtier to interrogate such a prisoner, which in practice amounts to the winged creature opening its captive's skull and devouring what lies inside.

# MORDANTS

**The cannibalistic wretches known as mordants flock towards Ghoul Kings and Archregents, drawn by the irresistible magnetism of the abhorrants' madness. Forming up in packs to better hunt their prey, they are more savage than soldier, yet in their minds they march in lockstep to war for the glory of their noble kingdom.**

## CRYPT HORRORS

Lumbering and snarling into battle come the Crypt Horrors. Their flesh stuck through with jagged bones and dripping blades, these are the knights of their court, armed not with sword and steed, but claw and fang. They are monstrous beasts, ineffably loyal and ever eager to serve their lord in battle, and they express their constancy through fits of feral rage and acts of gruesome slaughter.

Despite their hunched forms, Crypt Horrors loom above their smaller brethren, each one a monster of pale flesh and twisted bone. Hideously strong, they rip organs right out of their victims, stuffing shining handfuls of offal into their dripping maws. Crypt Horrors were once ghouls that were fed vampire blood by their Abhorrant Ghoul King, and as a result their bodies have grown enormous, becoming stronger and swifter through the power of dark sorcery.

In the depths of their delusion, Crypt Horrors believe themselves to be mounted defenders of the realm, charging into battle clad in shining plate. As befits their role within the court, they are often the first to the fight, sprinting out ahead of the king's foot soldiers to crash into the midst of the foe. Here, their supernatural resilience and prodigious strength are put to good use, each sweep of their claws ripping throats open and shattering shields. Return attacks have little effect, the Crypt Horrors' own bodies quickly healing mortal wounds, even closing around their enemy's blades. These regenerative powers are a gift of the abhorrant's blood that runs in their veins, though it comes at a price. Their muscles and bones are constantly twisting and growing, spines from their ribs and vertebrae forcing their way through flesh, just as their talons and teeth push their way free

of fingers and gums. Only the work of the king's Abattoir keeps their growth in check, the bones regularly harvested to make medals for the king's men.

Crypt Horrors are routinely honoured for their service by the king and his courtiers, and they will be offered tokens of the court's appreciation. Prized skulls, decaying limbs and crude bone weapons are presented to the Crypt Horrors as trophies, and the most decorated might rise in the ranks to become Crypt Haunters and take leadership of a Crypt Horror pack. Crypt Horrors lovingly care for these gifts, which they see as pennants, resplendent armour or swords. They may even claim such spoils in battle, and relieve their victims of burdens like their arms or spines. The Crypt Horror may shove its newly acquired prize, still dripping with gore, through its skin or down its maw, or it may turn it against its former owner.

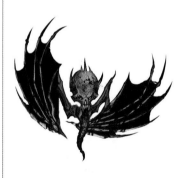

## CRYPT FLAYERS

Crypt Flayers haunt the night, soaring through the sky like dark shadows above the battlefield. With keen eyes they pick out enemies in the gloom below, and their powerful nostrils latch onto the waft of fear. Swooping down with lightning speed, they snatch hapless victims off their feet, sinking their fangs into their captives even as they soar back into the air.

Crypt Flayers are born when the blood of monsters flows freely on the feasting table. On such fell nights, an Abhorrant Ghoul King might bestow a horrific transformation upon his servants. The deranged sovereign mixes his blood with Terrorgheist flesh and necrotised fluids, and those ghouls who sup on this concoction are twisted into new and terrifying shapes. A layer of writhing skin grows around the ghoul, and then from this fleshy sack a Crypt Flayer emerges into the realms.

After being reborn in this way, the enchantments bestowed upon the Crypt Flayers take full hold, transforming them into dark predators. Growing huge and twisted, Crypt Flayers gain the added nightmare growth of leathery wings. Their claws elongate, spines burst from their backs and their eyes glow stronger to pierce the murk and gloom of battle. No longer bound to the earth, they take to the skies as airborne scouts and warriors for the court. Ferocious killers, Crypt Flayers wheel through the air above their king's domain, sniffing the wind for juicy hunting grounds. Those of who are seen as most noble by their cannibal kindred are called Crypt Infernals – taller and stronger than the rest, they lead from the front as shining examples to their 'men'.

Whether seen through a lens of madness or in all their rotting glory, none that have faced them can doubt that Crypt Flayers are brutally efficient in battle. They are darkly blessed by the tainted Terrorgheist flesh they have ingested, and in their chests dwells a measure of the undead beast's capacity to unleash a mind-shredding shriek. With their mouths impossibly wide they let loose a chorus of chilling howls, as if the gates to a dozen underworlds had been flung open at once. Their victims' blood turns to ice in their veins and terror grips their hearts as the sonic assault washes over them. The Crypt Flayers then dart from the sky like harpoons of sharpened bone, running any remaining warriors through and lifting them off the ground, screeching in exaltation as their prey dies screaming in a spray of gore. As they take back to the sky, the pack fights among themselves for the largest and most gruesome keepsake to lay at their king's throne.

Crypt Flayers are regarded with awe and adulation by their mordant kin. It is viewed as a good omen to see one or more of these winged beings circling above an expedition, and their shrill screams fill each ghoul with pride to be in their king's court. The Crypt Flayers themselves believe they are borne aloft by enchanted pinions gifted to them by their sovereign, or are convinced they are riders mounted upon magnificent flying beasts. In the minds of other mordants, Crypt Flayers are hallowed warriors, having been daubed with sacred oils by their king. Their howls do not sound like life-rending shrieks, but holy verses intoned with pious authority.

## CRYPT GHOULS

Reeking drool drips from gaping mouths, mixing with the blood and scraps of flesh that are lodged between rows of rotting fangs. As one, the Crypt Ghouls howl and hiss their adulation for their king, even as they scuttle into battle at his command. Their chipped talons tear at the ground, their maws stretch wider in eager anticipation of the feast to come. Then, with an explosion of insane ferocity, they crash into the enemy lines.

Ghoul is a word known in almost every corner of the Mortal Realms. These are the vile creatures who make up the majority of a court's seething armies, and they have an appetite for flesh that is both repulsive and insatiable. Once afflicted by the abhorrant's curse, the ghouls do not see themselves as monsters, and the longer they serve their monarch, the stronger their madness becomes. They

begin to believe that they are stout foot soldiers of the king's court or keen-eyed scouts ranging ahead of his armies, though in truth they are still a cannibal horde of ragged and hungry monsters. Anyone caught in the path of a ghoul pack has but two choices: fight or be devoured. Once the king has set them on an enemy's trail, the flesh-eating creatures will not rest until they have returned to their master laden with dripping slabs of freshly harvested meat.

Crypt Ghouls are especially deadly in large numbers. A single creature will take its time feeding, stripping the flesh from a victim until it has reduced its prey to little more than a bare skeleton. However, as soon as there is competition for its

meal it flies into a frenzy, swiftly ripping hunks of meat from one enemy before moving on, eager to avoid sharing its war spoils with its demented kin.

Utterly devoted to their abhorrant master, Crypt Ghouls will brave death without hesitation. Any craven parts of their soul have been extinguished by the madness of their king, and they fight like rabid beasts, often dying to the last rather than displeasing their lord. In those rare instances when a ghoul does turn to flight, their kin swiftly drag them down. Such is the fate for cowards in the Flesh-eater Courts, where the courageous fight on in their king's favour, their bellies filled with the flesh of the weak.

# MENAGERIE

**In crude pens fashioned from colossal bones the Ghoul Kings keep the decrepit beasts of their menageries. Some abhorrants use their favourite undead pets as mounts to bear them into battle, whereas others simply unleash these flying monstrosities and allow them to tear through the opposing army at will.**

## ROYAL TERRORGHEISTS

Nightmarish beings born of the oldest Shyishan sorceries, Terrorgheists are undead monsters bound to the will of the abhorrant kings. At some point they were proud creatures of flesh and blood, but now they are heaving carcasses of rotting muscle and cracked bone, with a vampiric thirst equal to that of their masters. They soar over the throng of combat, their otherworldly senses seeking great foes to slay. Especially large enemies are snatched up, the Terrorgheist sinking its fangs into warm flesh and drinking deep. The foul creatures strengthen visibly as they wolf down their prey, their ragged flesh regenerating and wounds disappearing, to the dismay of their enemies.

A Terrorgheist's fangs are far from its deadliest weapon, and the beast's scream is as unmistakable as it is devastating. A high-pitched wail, it cuts across the battlefield, shattering the minds of nearby prey. Those not slain outright are reduced to gibbering wrecks, howling as blood runs freely from their ears and eyes.

## ROYAL ZOMBIE DRAGONS

The sky shudders to the beat of leathery wings when a Zombie Dragon descends upon its prey. As the stench of the beast washes over the enemy, the air becomes chill, for the aura of death around the undead dragon is strong. Its eye sockets glimmer with what appears to be a ghostly intelligence. Yet this is but an illusion created by the vast quantities of dark energy used to animate such a creature, and it is raw amethyst magic that emanates from the monster's skull. Only the strongest wielders of necromantic power can command these creatures, and without their will the beasts are swiftly rendered inert once more.

The darkness that animates a Zombie Dragon is never more evident than when it expels its breath, spewing it forth as a coiling cloud of pestilential death magic. This killing miasma withers flesh and corrodes the soul, instantly sapping the life from living beings. In its wake are left husks where once were soldiers.

# INSANE MANIFESTATIONS

Like all vampiric creatures, abhorrants draw their magic from the deathly energies of Shyish. Since the necroquake, many of their most powerful conjurations persist as undying spells, blighting the landscape in perpetuity or feeding off madness and fear as they carve their way across the realms.

## CORPSEMARE STAMPEDE

With a bellowed word, an abhorrant sends tendrils of sickly light lancing from his outstretched fingers. These beams of necrotic energy plunge into the earth, causing the ground to heave violently upwards until it cracks open and a quintet of rotting horses bursts forth. These undead steeds charge headlong into whatever hapless victims stand before them, crushing packed ranks of infantry beneath the thrash of their gore-encrusted hooves.

To the abhorrant who summoned it, a Corpsemare Stampede appears as a herd of graceful beasts formed of purest light. He sees them surging forwards in radiant splendour, driven by inherent nobility to lay low all who are wicked of heart. Mordants who behold the stampede are overcome with a sense of humility, for they know that the judgement of the enchanted beings is levelled at them, just as it is against their enemies, and that the beasts will deliver the king's fury upon them if they are found wanting.

Yet in truth there is no such rhyme or reason to the stampede's path. The insane sorcery that animates the corpsemares causes them to wheel and charge in erratic patterns, barrelling through rows of screaming warriors in one direction before switching course and bolting towards a fresh set of bodies. A blood-chilling whine issues from their skeletal jaws as they move across the battlefield, and with every hoof-fall comes a deafening crack of dark magic. Even the most dauntless shield wall cannot hold them back – armour crumples, bones shatter and organs burst as the corpsemares ride over their victims. Any attempt to strike them down proves utterly fruitless, for the ragged flesh of the horses' bodies sloughs away rapidly, only to be replaced with the gore of those crushed into the mud beneath them.

## CHALICE OF USHORAN

Before his corruption, Ushoran crafted an ensorcelled goblet with which he could bestow blessings upon his loyal subjects. Wrought from gold and silver, and encrusted with realmstone from the lands he conquered, it was said that this goblet drew into itself the finest vintages from each liberated domain, and in this way never ran dry. Those who supped this wine were imbued with a portion of their king's majesty, and could stay the hand of death with a mere command. Though this famed chalice has been lost to the ravages of time, abhorrants who invoke the name of the Carrion King can summon its simulacrum to the battlefield.

When manifested, the Chalice of Ushoran appears as a colossal construction of polished bone. Each of the skulls that form its rim is of a pretender who was slaughtered at the hand of the Carrion King, and the cup overflows not with wine, but with the blood and viscera of those butchered on the battlefield. The screaming spirits of the slain bear the chalice aloft, and with every fresh kill their gore rises higher within the receptacle, overflowing and drenching nearby Flesh-eaters. Bathed in this necromantic harvest, wounds seal closed and severed limbs regrow, and even those mordants who have been cut down may rise to fight once more.

## CADAVEROUS BARRICADE

Those Flesh-eaters who believe themselves to be especially pious may call upon ancestral spirits to aid them in battle. By invoking oaths sworn many centuries ago by civilisations that bowed before Ushoran, an abhorrant gives life to the buried dead that served his sovereign in bygone times. From long-forgotten tombs they emerge, rising up to the battlefield so that they may once more fight for the cause of their lord.

In the eyes of an abhorrant, the dead upon whom they have called manifest as mighty spectral warriors, clad in ornate armour and carrying broad shields. The spiritual guardians form up into a tight defensive position, and from within their ranks rises a barrier of impenetrable light. They were once defenders of Ushoran's empire, charged with protecting the walls of his keeps and castles for all eternity, and they diligently carry on this duty from beyond the grave. Silent and dauntless, they stand firm as the enemy charges, holding back waves of foes whilst shielding the abhorrant's armies from hails of arrows and bolts.

But these spectral defenders are an illusion seen only in the insane minds of the Flesh-eaters. It is not gleaming warriors that rise from the grave, but mouldering corpses imbued with mindless hunger and rage. As they claw their way up through the ground they drag with them twisted remnants of the ancient civilisation of which they were once a part – rusted palisades covered with gore and barbed fences that surrounded mass graves. Foetid blood spills forth from the wound in the earth, releasing a nauseating fume into the air, while cadaverous hands grasp at any foes foolish enough to stray within reach of the moaning dead.

*A seething throng of Flesh-eaters from the Morgaunt Grand Court descend upon the Ironjawz army that has invaded their bone-strewn homeland.*

# GRISLY PAGEANTRY

With their filth-encrusted flesh, gore-covered claws and macabre accoutrements, Flesh-eater Courts Citadel Miniatures are a horrific presence on any tabletop. Here we present a showcase of these miniatures, expertly painted by Games Workshop's very own 'Eavy Metal Team and Design Studio army painters.

*An Abhorrant Archregent perched atop his Charnel Throne surveys the cannibalistic forces gathered around him, his mere presence serving to twist their deranged perception of reality even further.*

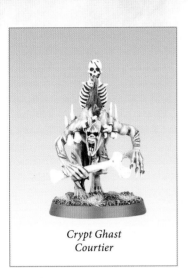

*Crypt Ghast
Courtier*

*Crypt Ghouls*

*Mordants surround their greenskin foes on the battlefield, moving in to rip their prey limb from limb before carrying away the tattered pieces of flesh as offerings to their Ghoul King.*

Abhorrant Ghoul King

Varghulf Courtier

Abhorrant Ghoul King on Royal Terrorgheist

Hollowmourne
Crypt Flayer

Morgaunt
Crypt Flayer

Abhorrant Archregent

*Crimson gore soaks into the sun-parched earth as an Abhorrant Archregent leads his maddened followers to battle against the rage-filled servants of the Blood God.*

*Crypt Horrors*

*Closing in on their prey, snarling packs of Crypt Ghouls and Crypt Horrors surge through the miasmal mists, their mouths agape in anticipation of the feast to come.*

*Seeing themselves as crusading knights, Flesh-eaters of the Hollowmourne Grand Court barrel headlong towards the Stormcast Eternals' defensive line, howling their gibberish war cries as they charge.*

# MANIFEST INSANITY

*Gristlegore Crypt Horror*     *Blisterskin Crypt Flayer*     *Shyishan Crypt Horror*

The appearance of each Flesh-eater Court is a reflection of its abhorrants' madness. Cannibals see themselves dressed in the brightly coloured armour and fine regalia of their domain, and through dark magics their skin and muscles take on these colours.

*Ghyranite Crypt Horror*

*Hyshian Crypt Horror*

*Ulguan Crypt Horror*

*Morgaunt Flesh-eaters race across the wind-whipped plain towards their foe, their madness blinding them to the illusory magics of the Disciples of Tzeentch.*

Corpsemare Stampede

Chalice of Ushoran

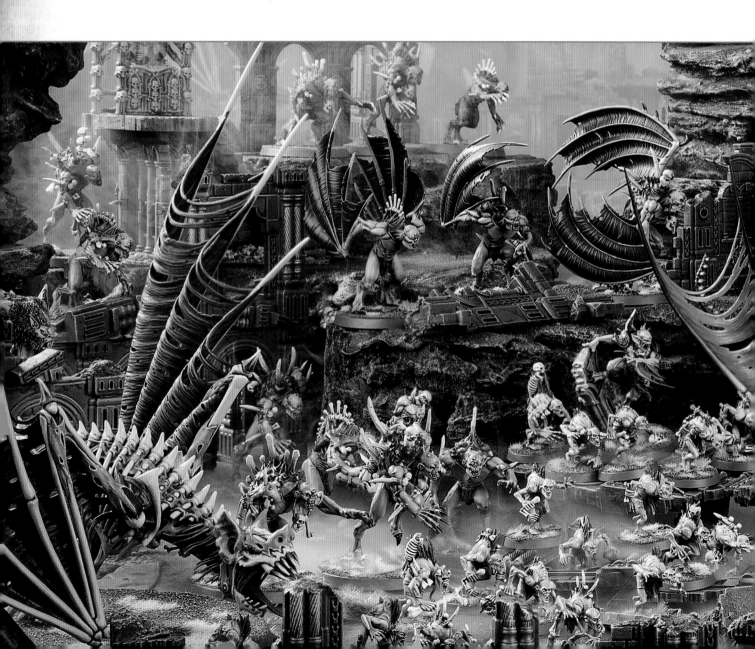

*Cadaverous Barricade*

Skaven of the Clans Skryre burrow up into Chamon to plunder a fabled empire, only to find the snarling ranks of a Flesh-eater Court waiting for them amongst the ancient ruins.

# DEATHLY REVENANTS

**Flesh-eaters gather in the crumbling ruins of long-dead civilisations, drawn by the call of the abhorrants and bound by their madness into armies of cannibal warriors. There are many ways to collect a Flesh-eater Courts army, and this spread offers one example of how a hungering horde can be mustered for war.**

When collecting a Warhammer Age of Sigmar army, it's a good idea to have a plan. How you decide which units to include in your Flesh-eater Courts army might be based on the look of the models, how you envision them performing during a tabletop battle, or could follow a narrative found in a battletome or even one of your own invention. There is no single right way to collect your army, only the way you deem best. The goal is the same – to field a ravenous Flesh-eater Courts army that is ready for action! Here is how we assembled the collection shown below.

The leader of this army is Visk the Blood-drinker, a mighty Abhorrant Archregent. Not only is he a visually impressive general for the army, he is also a savage combatant who can use deathly magic to strengthen his allies and rip apart his foes. At his side is his royal lieutenant, King Manglemaw, an Abhorrant Ghoul King who rides a monstrous Terrorgheist into battle. Both Visk and Manglemaw have the ability to summon their insane minions directly into the thick of combat, allowing them to bolster the strength of their army when needed.

Commanding the right flank is the Varghulf Courtier known as the Marquis de Flense. Ardently loyal to his Ghoul King and his Archregent, he flies above the battlefield accompanied by an escort of Crypt Flayers, seeking out the thickest clots of enemy warriors upon whom to sate his bloodlust. Meanwhile, on the ground below, a Crypt Haunter – granted the title of Lord Slendernail by his abhorrant for his feats in combat – leads his Crypt Horrors in loping charges against the foe, tearing through the ranks of opposing armies with gruesome enthusiasm.

On the opposite flank, the darkly charismatic Crypt Haunter Courtier, Lord Scabmire, howls gibberish commands to the cannibals he leads. A unit of Crypt Horrors serves as his battlefield bodyguard, slaughtering any enemies that draw near their lord, or roaming out alongside him in search of fresh prey. Arrayed in front of Scabmire are four units of Crypt Ghouls, the foot soldiers of the court. They race forwards in heaving packs to overwhelm the enemy, their blood-encrusted claws tearing at the ground and their mouths agape in anticipation of the feast to come. They are the true core of the army, in terms of both the carnage they can unleash and in the visual impact they have on the tabletop.

Bringing up the rear of Visk's insane throng are more winged creatures of the court – nightmarish flyers that can hunt the skies above the battlefield. A Royal Terrorgheist and a Royal Zombie Dragon drawn from the Ghoul King's menagerie provide an intimidating presence on either flank, while behind them are two more units of Crypt Flayers. All of these highly mobile and deadly creatures can swoop swiftly to wherever they are needed, flocking towards the front lines to add their savagery to an assault, or hunting down and picking off lone units.

As a whole, this Flesh-eater Courts army presents a collector and painter with a variety of gruesome creatures, and with an assortment of heroes, monsters and mordant troops, it also serves as a competitive tabletop force offering many exciting gaming options.

1. Abhorrant Archregent
2. Abhorrant Ghoul King on Royal Terrorgheist
3. Varghulf Courtier
4. Crypt Haunter Courtier
5. Crypt Horrors
6. Crypt Horrors
7. Crypt Flayers
8. Crypt Flayers
9. Crypt Flayers
10. Crypt Ghouls
11. Crypt Ghouls
12. Crypt Ghouls
13. Crypt Ghouls
14. Royal Terrorgheist
15. Royal Zombie Dragon

*'These wretches are a blight on our beloved homelands, and must be slaughtered one and all. Join with me, my countrymen, as I show these curs the resolve of true nobility.'*
- Visk the Blood-drinker

# PAINTING YOUR FLESH-EATER COURTS

**Whether you have never painted a Citadel Miniature in your life or are a master of the brush with decades of experience, the prospect of painting a Flesh-eater Courts army offers an exciting challenge. On the following pages you will find stage-by-stage guides to get you started, with tips and examples from the experts.**

There is nothing like the sight of a fully painted army of Citadel Miniatures. There is real satisfaction to be had in adding colour to your collection, teasing out the finely sculpted details, making your miniatures your own, and creating a unified force. After all, one painted model looks great, but an entire army brought together through shared colours, iconography and grim heraldry is even more fantastic.

There's no right or wrong way to go about painting your collection of miniatures. Some people revel in treating each miniature as a work of art, lavishing attention on every millimetre of every model and painstakingly crafting scenic bases. Others prefer a far simpler approach with basic but consistent paint jobs that allow them to quickly complete

legions of finished warriors. And, of course, there is plenty of middle ground for those that enjoy painting their troops but want to devote special attention to key figures such as heroes and monsters. Again, there is no one way to paint, just the way that works best for you. In the end, the goal is to field a fully painted court on the tabletop – and with many insane, snarling cannibals in its throng, their fangs and claws encrusted with viscera, a Flesh-eater Courts army can be truly terrifying to behold.

Before painting your models, you'll first need to assemble them. To begin with, we suggest you follow the advice given in the construction booklet provided with your models. The following pages provide inspiration for how you

can paint your constructed models, including colour schemes for many of the most infamous Grand Courts, but for in depth painting tutorials we recommend visiting our Warhammer TV YouTube channel.

## WARHAMMER TV

Warhammer TV's painting tutorials have insights for everyone, as they show you how to paint Citadel Miniatures from start to finish. The guides are available for free on games-workshop.com, and can also be watched via the Warhammer TV YouTube channel. Why not take a moment to check them out?

## MORGAUNT GRAND COURT

**1**

Apply a basecoat of Corax White Spray to the entire miniature.

**2**

Shade skin areas with a 1:1 mixture of Agrax Earthshade and Lahmian Medium.

**3**

Layer with Pallid Wych Flesh.

**4**

Use White Scar to apply highlights to raised areas.

### BLOODY HANDS

Apply Carroburg Crimson over the finished skin.

### BRASS

**Base:** Fulgurite Copper
**Shade:** Agrax Earthshade
**Layer:** Fulgurite Copper
**Highlight:** Stormhost Silver

### MOUTH

**Base:** Rhinox Hide
**Teeth:** Screaming Skull
**Tongue:** Screamer Pink
followed by Pink Horror

### CLAWS & SPINES

**Base:** Rhinox Hide
**Highlight:** Skrag Brown,
then Balor Brown, then
Screaming Skull

## WING MEMBRANE

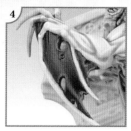

Apply a basecoat of Khorne Red to the wing membrane.

Wash with a 1:1 mixture of Druchii Violet and Lahmian Medium.

Layer with Wazdakka Red.

Highlight the tattered edges with Squig Orange.

## ALTERNATE WING COLOURS

Apply a basecoat of Karak Stone and then shade with Seraphim Sepia mixed with Lahmian Medium in a 1:1 ratio. Layer Karak Stone on the raised sections of the membrane, then apply Abaddon Black mixed with Lahmian Medium in a 1:1 ratio in progressive thin layers to build up the darkened effect.

Apply a basecoat of Khorne Red, wash with a 1:1 mixture of Druchii Violet and Lahmian Medium, then layer with Wazdakka Red. Highlight the edges with Squig Orange followed by Fire Dragon Bright. Finally, paint in the pattern using Abaddon Black with Mechanicus Standard Grey highlights.

Apply a basecoat of Ushabti Bone, shade with a 1:1 mixture of Seraphim Sepia and Lahmian Medium, then layer with Ushabti Bone on the upper sections of the membrane. Highlight the raised areas with Screaming Skull. Paint in the pattern with a thin coat of Xereus Purple.

## BONES

Apply a basecoat of Rakarth Flesh, shade with Seraphim Sepia, then layer with Rakarth Flesh lengthwise down the bone. Finish with a highlight of Pallid Wych Flesh.

## EXPOSED MUSCULATURE

Use Khorne Red as a basecoat, then add a Nuln Oil Gloss wash for a wet appearance. Highlight with Evil Sunz Scarlet on the upper sections of the muscle, followed by a final highlight of Fire Dragon Bright.

## FUR

Apply a basecoat of Khorne Red, then use thin coats of Nuln Oil to build up shade on the lower areas of the fur. Drybrush the upper areas with Evil Sunz Scarlet, followed by a fine highlight with Kislev Flesh.

## BLISTERSKIN GRAND COURT

1

Spray with Corax White, then apply a basecoat of Squig Orange.

2

Apply shade using Carroburg Crimson.

3

Layer with Cadian Fleshtone.

4

Use Karak Stone to highlight raised areas.

### BURNT FLESH

Stipple Abaddon Black over finished skin to achieve a burnt effect.

### PALE CHEST

(Over finished skin) **Base:** Rakarth Flesh; **Wash:** 1:1 Druchii Violet and Lahmian Medium; **Highlight:** Rakarth Flesh layer; Pallid Wych Flesh

### PURPLE TO BLACK WING

**Base:** Screamer Pink
**Drybrush:** Kislev Flesh
**Layer and stippling:** Abaddon Black
**Shade:** Nuln Oil Gloss

## GRISTLEGORE GRAND COURT

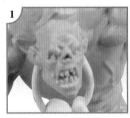

1

Spray with Corax White, then apply a basecoat of Celestra Grey.

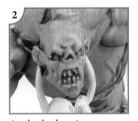

2

Apply shade using Coelia Greenshade.

3

Layer with Celestra Grey.

4

Use Ulthuan Grey to highlight raised areas.

### AMBER BONES

**Base:** XV-88
**Shade:** Seraphim Sepia
**Layer:** Tau Light Ochre
**Highlight:** Screaming Skull

### BLOOD MARKINGS

Apply splatters of Blood for the Blood God over finished skin to make handprints.

### ROTTEN CORPSE

**Base:** Ogryn Camo
**Shade:** Athonian Camoshade
**Layer:** Ogryn Camo
**Highlight:** Pallid Wych Flesh

## HOLLOWMOURNE GRAND COURT

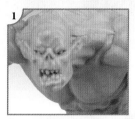

**1**

Spray with Corax White then apply a basecoat of Celestra Grey.

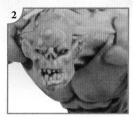

**2**

Apply shade using Athonian Camoshade.

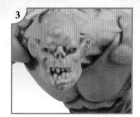

**3**

Layer with Administratum Grey.

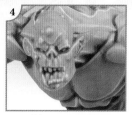

**4**

Use Ulthuan Grey to highlight raised areas.

### BLACKENED HIDE

Apply Incubi Darkness over finished skin around the base of the bones.

### RED WING

**Base:** Khorne Red
**Shade:** 1:1 Nuln Oil and Lahmian Medium
**Drybrush:** Wazdakka Red, then Kislev Flesh

### BOILS

Over finished skin, shade with Casandora Yellow, then apply a highlight of Ulthuan Grey.

### NECROTIC FLESH

Spray with Chaos Black, then apply a basecoat of Abaddon Black. Next use Mechanicus Standard Grey to lightly drybrush the raised areas. Then apply another drybrushed layer of Dawnstone. Then, using Administratum Grey, drybrush around the sores and open wounds.

### BASING YOUR FLESH-EATER COURT MINIATURES

Use bones from the Crypt Horrors kit, cut at random angles, and strew them around the base. After an undercoat of Chaos Black, apply Agrellan Earth followed by a drybrush of Mechanicus Standard Grey and a second drybrush of Dawnstone. Paint the bones using the guide on page 51, and apply random patches of Blood For The Blood God in thick coats to create the pools of blood.

Apply an undercoat of Chaos Black Spray to a Shattered Dominion base, followed by a basecoat of Stormvermin Fur, then shade with Athonian Camoshade and drybrush with Karak Stone. Next, scatter skulls from the Citadel Skulls basing kit around the edge in small piles: to paint them, follow the guide on page 51. Apply Blood For The Blood God in random splatter patterns to complete the gruesome effect.

# RAVENOUS HORDES

This battletome contains all of the rules you need to field your Flesh-eater Courts miniatures on the battlefields of the Mortal Realms, from a host of exciting allegiance abilities to a range of warscrolls and warscroll battalions. The rules are split into the following sections.

## ALLEGIANCE ABILITIES
This section describes the allegiance abilities available to a Flesh-eater Courts army. The rules for how to use the following allegiance abilities can be found in the core rules.

## BATTLE TRAITS
Abilities available to every unit in a Flesh-eater Courts army (pg 55).

## COMMAND TRAITS
Abilities available to the general of a Flesh-eater Courts army if it is a HERO (pg 56).

## ARTEFACTS OF POWER
Artefacts available to HEROES in a Flesh-eater Courts army (pg 57).

## SPELL LORES
Spells available to WIZARDS in a Flesh-eater Courts army (pg 58).

The following unique allegiance abilities are also available to a Flesh-eater Courts army. The rules for how to use these allegiance abilities can be found on the relevant pages.

## MOUNT TRAITS
Traits for the mounts ridden by HEROES in a Flesh-eater Courts army (pg 59).

## CHARNEL THRONE
Here you will find the rules and scenery warscroll for the Charnel Throne (pg 60-61).

## GRAND COURTS
Abilities for four of the most famous Flesh-eater Grand Courts (pg 62-65). These rules can be used by units in a Flesh-eater Courts army that have been given the appropriate keyword (see the Grand Courts Battle Trait, opposite).

## BATTLEPLANS
This section includes a new narrative battleplan that can be played with a Flesh-eater Courts army (pg 66-67).

## PATH TO GLORY
This section contains rules for using your Flesh-eater Courts collection in Path to Glory campaigns (pg 68-71).

## WARSCROLLS
This section includes all of the warscrolls you will need to play games of Warhammer Age of Sigmar with your Flesh-eater Courts miniatures.

There are three types of warscroll included in this section:

## WARSCROLL BATTALIONS
These are formations made up of several Flesh-eater Courts units that combine their strengths to gain powerful new abilities (pg 72-75).

## WARSCROLLS
A warscroll for each unit is included here. The rules for using a Flesh-eater Courts unit, along with its characteristics and abilities, are detailed on its warscroll (pg 76-85).

## ENDLESS SPELL WARSCROLLS
There are three endless spell warscrolls that detail the rules for unique and powerful spells that can be summoned by FLESH-EATER COURTS WIZARDS (pg 86-87). The rules for playing games with endless spells can be found in the *Warhammer Age of Sigmar Core Book*, and in *Warhammer Age of Sigmar: Malign Sorcery*.

## PITCHED BATTLE PROFILES
This section contains Pitched Battle profiles for the units, warscroll battalions and endless spells in this book (pg 88).

## ALLIES
This section has a list of the allies a Flesh-eater Courts army can include (pg 88).

# ALLEGIANCE ABILITIES
## BATTLE TRAITS

### RAVENOUS INSANITY

**DEATHLESS COURTIERS**
*When Flesh-eaters linger in the shadow of their stronger kin, their sundered flesh heals in an instant.*

Roll a dice each time you allocate a wound or mortal wound to a friendly **FLESH-EATER COURTS** unit wholly within 12" of a friendly **FLESH-EATER COURTS HERO**. On a 6 that wound or mortal wound is negated.

**GRAND COURTS**
*Some courts are infamous across the Mortal Realms for their depravity and slaughter.*

After you have chosen the Flesh-eater Courts allegiance for your army, you can choose one of the following Grand Court keywords. All **FLESH-EATER COURTS** units in your army gain that keyword. You cannot pick or roll a delusion (see below) for a Grand Court, but all units with that keyword benefit from the extra abilities detailed for that Grand Court.

- **MORGAUNT** (pg 62)   - **HOLLOWMOURNE** (pg 63)
- **BLISTERSKIN** (pg 64)   - **GRISTLEGORE** (pg 65)

**COURTS OF DELUSION**
*The warriors of a Flesh-eater Court believe themselves noble soldiers serving a glorious king.*

Before you select your general's command trait, pick one of the delusions to the right for the army to have. Alternatively, you can roll a dice to randomly determine the delusion the army has. The delusion applies to all friendly **FLESH-EATER COURTS** units for the duration of the battle, even if the general is slain (if you must select a new general during the battle, do not generate a new delusion for the army).

**COMMAND ABILITY**
**Feeding Frenzy:** *As the court closes upon its enemies, the nobility signal for the feasting to begin.*

You can use this command ability after a friendly **FLESH-EATER COURTS** unit has fought in the combat phase for the first time and is wholly within 12" of a friendly **FLESH-EATER COURTS HERO**, or wholly within 18" of a friendly **FLESH-EATER COURTS HERO** that is a general. If you do so, that unit can immediately make a pile-in move and then attack with all of the melee weapons it is armed with for a second time. You cannot pick the same unit to benefit from this ability more than once per phase.

| D6 | Delusion |
|----|----------|
| 1 | **Crusading Army:** *The wicked and impious must be ridden down wherever they are.* <br><br> Add 1 to run and charge rolls for friendly **FLESH-EATER COURTS** units. |
| 2 | **The Royal Hunt:** *It is a great honour to slay the largest quarry in preparation for the feast.* <br><br> You can re-roll hit rolls of 1 and wound rolls of 1 for attacks made by friendly **FLESH-EATER COURTS** units that target a **MONSTER**. |
| 3 | **The Feast Day:** *All members of the court make merry on this day of celebration.* <br><br> Once per turn, you can use the Feeding Frenzy command ability without a command point being spent. |
| 4 | **A Matter of Honour:** *The enemy will repent only when their wretched leaders are dead.* <br><br> You can re-roll hit rolls of 1 for attacks made by friendly **FLESH-EATER COURTS** units that target a **HERO**. If the target is a general, you can re-roll wound rolls of 1 as well. |
| 5 | **The Grand Tournament:** *Noble warriors vie for the admiration of their king.* <br><br> You can re-roll hit rolls of 1 for attacks made by friendly **FLESH-EATER COURTS HEROES** other than your general. |
| 6 | **Defenders of the Realm:** *The sovereign's domain must be purged of evil.* <br><br> You can re-roll save rolls of 1 for friendly **FLESH-EATER COURTS** units that have at least half their models wholly within their own territory. |

---

*Muster Abilities: Several Flesh-eater Courts units have Muster abilities, such as Muster Royal Guard (pg 82), that allow you to return slain models to a unit. If you use a Muster ability, set up the returning models one at a time within 1" of a model from the unit they are returning to (this can be a model returned earlier that phase). The models can only be set up within 3" of an enemy unit if any models from their unit are already within 3" of that enemy unit.*

# COMMAND TRAITS

## ROYALTY

**ABHORRANT HEROES** only.

| D6 | Command Trait |
|----|---------------|

**1 Bringer of Death:** *This general sees every enemy as a wretch that must be put out of its misery.*

You can re-roll wound rolls for attacks made by this general.

**2 Frenzied Flesh-eater:** *The sight of a bleeding foe spurs this ghoulish creature into a frenzy.*

You can re-roll hit and wound rolls for attacks made by this general if there are any enemy models that have suffered any wounds within 3" of this general.

**3 Savage Beyond Reason:** *The fury of battle drives this general into an intense rage.*

If the unmodified hit roll for an attack made with a melee weapon by this general is 6, that attack inflicts 2 hits on the target instead of 1. Make a wound and save roll for each hit.

**4 Majestic Horror:** *The champion's grim regality draws countless cannibalistic warriors to his banner.*

If this general is chosen as the model that uses a command ability that summons **FLESH-EATER COURTS** models to the battlefield, they can use it without a command point having to be spent.

**5 Dark Wizardry:** *An aura of necromantic energy hangs thick around this creature.*

Add 1 to casting, dispelling and unbinding rolls for this general.

**6 Completely Delusional:** *The followers of this general see all that is in his mind's eye.*

Once per battle, if this general has not been slain, you can pick a new delusion in your hero phase to replace the original delusion you chose for your army (see page 55).

## NOBILITY

**COURTIER HEROES** only.

| D6 | Command Trait |
|----|---------------|

**1 Bringer of Death:** *This general sees every enemy as a wretch to be put out of their misery.*

You can re-roll wound rolls for attacks made by this general.

**2 Frenzied Flesh-eater:** *The sight of a bleeding foe spurs this ghoulish creature into a frenzy.*

You can re-roll hit and wound rolls for attacks made by this general if there are any enemy models that have suffered any wounds within 3" of this general.

**3 Savage Beyond Reason:** *The fury of battle drives this general into an intense rage.*

If the unmodified hit roll for an attack made with a melee weapon by this general is 6, that attack inflicts 2 hits on the target instead of 1. Make a wound and save roll for each hit.

**4 Hulking Brute:** *This courtier towers above others of its kin.*

Add 1 to this general's Wounds characteristic.

**5 Cruel Taskmaster:** *The warriors under this courtier's command instantly obey his summons.*

If this general uses a Muster ability you can re-roll the dice for this general that determine if slain models are returned to units (you must re-roll all of the dice).

**6 Dark Acolyte:** *This courtier has learnt some of the dark arts of wizardry.*

This general gains the **WIZARD** keyword and can cast and unbind spells in the same manner as an **ABHORRANT GHOUL KING** from the Abhorrant Ghoul King warscroll (pg 79).

# ARTEFACTS OF POWER

## ROYAL TREASURY
### Abhorrant Heroes only.

**D6  Artefact of Power**

1  **Signet of the First Court:** *Carved into the tangled sinew of this ancient ring is a deranged symbol that bestows the wearer with monstrous strength.*

   If the unmodified wound roll for an attack made by the bearer with a melee weapon is 6, add 1 to the damage inflicted by that attack.

2  **Splintervane Brooch:** *Those pierced by this shard of bone grow spiny protrusions from their flesh that absorb the flow of magic.*

   Subtract 1 from casting rolls for enemy **Wizards** while they are within 18" of the bearer.

3  **Blood-river Chalice:** *When the blood contained in this vessel is quaffed, the grisly fluid reknits even the most grievous wound.*

   Once per battle, at the start of your hero phase, the bearer can use this artefact. If they do so, heal up to D6 wounds allocated to the bearer.

4  **The Grim Garland:** *Formed from the skulls of kings and emperors, this morbid wreath evokes fear in even the bravest champion.*

   Subtract 2 from the Bravery characteristic of enemy units while they are within 6" of the bearer.

5  **The Dermal Robe:** *Once the skin of a powerful sorcerer, this cloak can only be donned by eating the current wearer out of it.*

   Add 1 to casting, dispelling and unbinding rolls for the bearer.

6  **Heart of the Gargant:** *This quivering slab of flesh still beats with the strength of the gargant from which it was torn, and each bite bestows colossal might.*

   Once per battle, at the start of the combat phase, the bearer can use this artefact. If they do so, you can re-roll failed wound rolls for the bearer and their mount in that phase.

## NOBLE HEIRLOOMS
### Courtier Heroes only.

**D6  Artefact of Power**

1  **Keening Bone:** *After this gnarled club has been hurled at an enemy, it will return to the hand of the last fiend to have tasted its juicy marrow.*

   Pick one of the bearer's melee weapons. Increase the Range characteristic of that weapon to 3".

2  **Medal of Madness:** *This gruesome badge is staked to the chest and allows the bearer to speak with the voice of their abhorrant.*

   Once per battle round, the bearer can use a command ability on their warscroll without a command point being spent, and they are treated as if they were a general when they do so.

3  **The Flayed Pennant:** *This dripping flag sends denizens of the courts into a frenzy.*

   You can re-roll charge rolls for friendly **Flesh-eater Courts** units wholly within 12" of the bearer.

4  **Carrion Wand:** *The thigh bone of this Ghoul King still carries a portion of his mad magic.*

   In your hero phase, the bearer can attempt to cast the Arcane Bolt spell as if they were a **Wizard**. If the bearer is a **Wizard**, add 1 to the casting roll when they attempt to cast Arcane Bolt instead.

5  **The Fleshform Raiment:** *This cloak gives the wearer the form of their enemies' deepest nightmares.*

   Subtract 1 from the Bravery characteristic of enemy units while they are within 3" of the bearer.

6  **The Bilious Decanter:** *The fluid in this offal flask fills the drinker with unquenchable rage.*

   Once per battle, at the start of the combat phase, the bearer can use this artefact. If they do so, add 2 to the Attacks characteristic of the bearer's melee weapons in that phase.

# SPELL LORES

You can choose or roll for one of the following spells for each **Wizard** in a Flesh-eater Courts army.

---

### LORE OF MADNESS

**D6   Spell**

**1   Bonestorm:** *The wizard summons a swirling whirlwind of splintered bone to slice through his enemies.*

Bonestorm has a casting value of 5. If successfully cast, roll a dice for each enemy unit within 12" of the caster. On a 2+ that unit suffers 1 mortal wound.

**2   Spectral Host:** *The mage intones a prayer to their forebears, summoning a flurry of gheists that lifts their allies high in the air and carries them forwards before bringing them safely back to the ground.*

Spectral Host has a casting value of 6. If successfully cast, pick 1 friendly unit wholly within 12" of the caster that is visible to them. That unit can fly until your next hero phase. If that unit can already fly, until your next hero phase it can run and still charge in the same turn. If the casting roll was 10 or more, you can pick up to 3 friendly units to be affected by the spell instead of 1.

**3   Monstrous Vigour:** *The wizard summons forth a burst of sustaining energy, allowing a grievously wounded creature to fight with renewed strength.*

Monstrous Vigour has a casting value of 5. If successfully cast, pick 1 friendly **Flesh-eater Courts Monster** within 24" of the caster that is visible to them. Until your next hero phase, when you look up a value on that **Monster**'s damage table, that **Monster** is treated as if it has suffered 0 wounds.

**4   Miasmal Shroud:** *The wizard calls forth a pale mist that engulfs the foe, making it impossible for the enemy to breathe or see their foes.*

Miasmal Shroud has a casting value of 5. If successfully cast, pick 1 enemy unit within 18" of the caster that is visible to them and roll 3 dice. For each 5+ that unit suffers 1 mortal wound. In addition, if you rolled a triple, subtract 1 from hit and wound rolls for that unit until your next hero phase. If you rolled a double, subtract 1 from hit rolls only for that unit until your next hero phase.

**5   Deranged Transformation:** *The spellcaster causes the limbs of a nearby pack to bulge and lengthen, allowing the creatures to charge forwards at a furious pace.*

Deranged Transformation has a casting value of 6. If successfully cast, pick 1 friendly unit with a Wounds characteristic of up to 6 that is wholly within 24" of the caster and visible to them. Add that unit's Wounds characteristic to its Move characteristic until your next hero phase. For example, if the unit had a Wounds characteristic of 6, you would add 6" to its Move characteristic. If the casting roll was 10 or more, you can pick up to 3 friendly units to be affected by the spell instead of 1.

**6   Blood Feast:** *The caster draws out the life essence of nearby foes and uses it to heal the injured warriors of their court.*

Blood Feast has a casting value of 7. If successfully cast, pick 1 enemy unit within 12" of the caster that is visible to them, and a friendly **Flesh-eater Courts** unit within 6" of that enemy unit. The enemy unit suffers D3 mortal wounds. If the casting roll was 10 or more, the enemy unit suffers D6 mortal wounds instead of D3 mortal wounds.

Then, for each mortal wound that was inflicted on the enemy unit, you can heal 1 wound allocated to the friendly unit. If the friendly unit has a Wounds characteristic of 1, for each mortal wound that was inflicted on the enemy unit, you can return 1 slain model to the friendly unit instead.

# MOUNT TRAITS

If a Flesh-eater Courts army includes any **HEROES** mounted on a Royal Terrorgheist or Royal Zombie Dragon, one of those **HEROES** can have a mount trait. Declare which **HERO** has the mount trait: you can then choose or roll for a mount trait from the appropriate table. You can choose one extra **HERO** to have a mount trait for each warscroll battalion in your army. A **HERO** cannot have more than one mount trait.

## TERRORGHEIST TRAITS
**HERO** mounted on Royal Terrorgheist only.

| D6 | Mount Trait |
|---|---|
| 1 | **Deathly Fast:** *This monstrous creature strikes with terrifying swiftness.*<br><br>This model can run and still shoot in the same turn. |
| 2 | **Razor-clawed:** *Over the centuries, this beast's claws and fangs have been honed to a razor edge.*<br><br>Improve the Rend characteristic of this mount's melee weapons by 1. |
| 3 | **Horribly Infested:** *The bats that infest this deathly monster are especially ferocious.*<br><br>This model's Infested ability inflicts 3 mortal wounds instead of D3 mortal wounds. |
| 4 | **Horribly Resilient:** *This undead monster is nearly impossible to kill.*<br><br>This model's Royal Blood ability heals up to 3 wounds instead of up to D3 wounds. |
| 5 | **Gruesome Bite:** *Few can avoid the bites inflicted by this creature's fanged maw.*<br><br>You can re-roll failed hit rolls for attacks made with this mount's Fanged Maw. |
| 6 | **Devastating Scream:** *This Terrorgheist's death shriek can overwhelm even the bravest of foes.*<br><br>Add 1 to each of the Death Shriek values on this model's damage table. |

## ZOMBIE DRAGON TRAITS
**HERO** mounted on Royal Zombie Dragon only.

| D6 | Mount Trait |
|---|---|
| 1 | **Deathly Fast:** *This monstrous creature strikes with terrifying swiftness.*<br><br>This model can run and still shoot in the same turn. |
| 2 | **Razor-clawed:** *Over the centuries, this beast's claws and fangs have been honed to a razor edge.*<br><br>Improve the Rend characteristic of this mount's melee weapons by 1. |
| 3 | **Baneful Breath:** *The killing miasma that this beast breathes out is deadly beyond reason.*<br><br>You can re-roll wound rolls for attacks made with this model's Pestilential Breath. |
| 4 | **Horribly Resilient:** *This undead monster is nearly impossible to kill.*<br><br>This model's Royal Blood ability heals up to 3 wounds instead of up to D3 wounds. |
| 5 | **Necrotic Fangs:** *Flesh turns to dust when pierced by this creature's jagged teeth.*<br><br>You can re-roll the Damage characteristic roll for this model's Snapping Maw. |
| 6 | **Death From The Skies:** *This steed soars above its master's army, before swooping to attack.*<br><br>Instead of setting up this model on the battlefield, you can place it to one side and say that it is soaring in the skies in reserve. If you do so, at the end of your first movement phase, you must set up this unit on the battlefield more than 9" from any enemy units. |

# CHARNEL THRONE

Wherever the Flesh-eaters thrive in the Mortal Realms they raise up Charnel Thrones – morbid constructions that mark the domain of an abhorrant.

A Flesh-eater Courts army can include 1 **CHARNEL THRONE** terrain feature (see opposite).

After territories have been chosen but before armies are set up, you can set up the **CHARNEL THRONE** wholly within your territory, wholly within 12" of the edge of the battlefield, and more than 1" from any objectives or other terrain features.

If both players can set up a terrain feature before armies are set up, they must roll off, and the winner can choose the order in which the terrain features are set up.

*V*esver the Exquisite, Lord of Slaanesh, drove his daemonic mount up the hill, caressing the serpentine beast's flanks with the barbed heels of his greaves. He had carved a brutal path across the battlefield, slaughtering those Flesh-eaters that stood in his way, and though they had defaced his resplendent armour with their blood and sinew, he would soon make their Ghoul King pay for these transgressions.

As he reached the crest of the hill, Vesver plunged his quicksilver glaive through a pair of Ghouls. After the briefest pause to relish the sounds of their dying agonies, he looked ahead of him and at last saw the Ghoul King of the Flesh-eaters army. It was a truly grotesque creature – hulking, hunched and slavering, and it was perched atop a pile of decaying skulls and ribcages that had been stacked into a towering mockery of a throne. Vesver allowed himself to be overcome with disgust.

'Sssavage creature!' he bellowed. 'You cannot possibly comprehend the sssuffering that awaits–'

Vesver's tongue caught in his mouth – it felt mangled and misshapen. His eyes were still fixed on the grim throne, but where it had seemed a moment ago to be a crude construction, its true shape was beginning to form in his mind – broad panels of burnished gold, laced together with threads of fine silver. The king sitting in this throne was not a savage cannibal, but a being of pure radiance, dressed in flowing robes and possessed of undeniable majesty. Such was the glory of this sovereign that Vesver had to avert his eyes, and when he looked down he beheld his own withered form and the tattered rags in which he was garbed. Overcome with humility, he descended from his mount and dropped to his knees, prostrating himself before this transcendent monarch.

'Be still,' spoke the Ghoul King, its voice at once calm and commanding. 'I shall soon put an end to your wretched existence.'

● SCENERY WARSCROLL ●

# CHARNEL THRONE

Formed from the bones of those killed by an abhorrant's insane magic, a Charnel Throne exudes madness and necrotic energies. They are the seats of power for Archregents and Ghoul Kings, blazing beacons to mordants, and structures of abject horror for the enemies of the Flesh-eaters.

## DESCRIPTION
A Charnel Throne is a single terrain feature. It is an obstacle.

## SCENERY RULES
**Ghoulish Landmark:** *A Ghoul King's followers are inspired by the presence of a Charnel Throne.*

**FLESH-EATER COURTS** units treat this terrain feature as having the Inspiring scenery rule. All other units treat this terrain feature as having the Sinister scenery rule.

*Inspiring:* Add 1 to the Bravery characteristic of units while they are within 1" of any Inspiring terrain features.

*Sinister:* Subtract 1 from the Bravery characteristic of units while they are within 1" of any Sinister terrain features.

**Ruler of All He Surveys:** *When an abhorrant sits upon a Charnel Throne, his followers flock to his feet.*

An **ABHORRANT ARCHREGENT** that is within 1" of this terrain feature can use the Summon Imperial Guard command ability without a command point being spent. In addition, an **ABHORRANT GHOUL KING** that is within 1" of this terrain feature can use the Summon Men-at-arms command ability without a command point being spent.

| KEYWORDS | SCENERY, FLESH-EATER COURTS, CHARNEL THRONE |

# MORGAUNT GRAND COURT

**Driven by an unshakable belief in their long-dead chivalric codes, Flesh-eaters of the Morgaunt Grand Court surge out to devour all who encroach upon their domains. Their courts are amongst the oldest in the Mortal Realms, and they gather mordants to their tattered banners in overwhelming numbers.**

Flesh-eaters of the Morgaunt Grand Court believe themselves denizens of lush and fertile lands, and see all who encroach upon their territories as savage marauders. In their madness they hold to principles of nobility and honour, defending the weak and innocent whilst fighting to topple those they perceive as wicked. But in truth, the Morgaunt domains are vast corpse-strewn wastelands through which massed packs of Ghouls scamper, running down and butchering all those who are not under the sway of their abhorrant's delusion.

The Morgaunt nobility display a fanatical devotion to the Ghouls that follow them. Courtiers fight with unflagging vigour when surrounded by their subjects, believing themselves to be bold knights standing proud amidst their troops. So too do the teeming throngs of lesser mordants look to the larger and more crazed Flesh-eaters as exemplars, and in the presence of these vaunted figures they tear into their enemies with savage abandon. The grim charisma that the Morgaunt courtiers and abhorrants possess sees cannibalistic wretches drawn from far and wide to join their armies. Even in the thick of battle, fresh packs of Ghouls continue to scrabble towards the maddened calls of the nobility – an unending flow of claws and fangs with which to butcher even the largest opposing force.

## ABILITIES

**Bloody Loyalty:** *The courtiers and serfs of the Morgaunt Grand Court share a bond of loyalty and fight fiercely on each other's behalf.*

You can re-roll hit rolls of 1 for friendly **MORGAUNT COURTIER** units that are wholly within 12" of a friendly **MORGAUNT SERFS** unit. In addition, while a friendly **MORGAUNT SERFS** unit is wholly within 12" of a friendly **MORGAUNT COURTIER**, its Boundless Ferocity ability activates if the **SERFS** unit has 10 or more models.

## COMMAND ABILITY

**Heaving Masses:** *Morgaunt courts crush their enemies with wave after wave of pallid warriors.*

You can use this command ability when a friendly **MORGAUNT SERFS** unit is destroyed. If you do so, roll a dice. On a 4+ new unit identical to the one that was destroyed is added to your army. Set up the new unit wholly within 6" of the edge of the battlefield and more than 9" from any enemy models.

## COMMAND TRAIT

A **MORGAUNT** general must have this command trait instead of one listed on page 56.

**Savage Chivalry:** *The rulers of the Morgaunt Grand Court fight ferociously to protect the weak and unfortunate.*

You can re-roll hit rolls of 1 for this general while this general is within 12" of a friendly **MORGAUNT SERFS** unit.

## ARTEFACT OF POWER

The first **MORGAUNT HERO** to receive an artefact of power must be given the Decrepit Coronet.

**Decrepit Coronet:** *Wrought from ancient bone and stitched together with sinew, this gruesome crown is the ultimate symbol of Morgaunt sovereignty.*

Do not take battleshock tests for friendly **MORGAUNT** units while they are wholly within 12" of the bearer, or wholly within 18" of the bearer if the bearer is your general.

# HOLLOWMOURNE GRAND COURT

**The Hollowmourne Grand Court is formed of the wretched descendants of heavily armoured and mounted knights from Chamon. Their numbers are replete with hulking mordants who charge headlong into battle, eviscerating their enemies with brutal ease before gorging themselves on the mangled corpses.**

The madness of the Hollowmourne Grand Court is fuelled by a gnawing sense of unfulfilled duty. The ancestors of these Flesh-eaters swore oaths to their emperor to find the relics he buried across the Mortal Realms, and to keep them from the clutches of Chaos. The nature and location of these relics has long since been lost, but the Hollowmourne courts still rove from realm to realm, desperately seeking the vaults in which these treasures are buried and slaughtering all those who stand in their path.

Before their descent into insanity, the Knights of the Hollowmourne were mighty and steadfast warriors. Clad in Chamonic plate and borne to battle on horseback, they swept aside opposing armies of far greater size with their devastating charges. During the Age of Chaos, when their crusade to find the hidden relics was shattered, the knights were forced into acts of utter depravity – eating first their peasant servants and eventually even their faithful mounts. In their deranged state of mind, they see themselves as still crusading, riding out in armoured columns to cut down those who would despoil the vaults that they seek. The largest and most ferocious mordants lead the charge, their bodies having grown to enormous proportions from feasting on the flesh of their enemies.

## ABILITIES

**Shattering Charge:** *The largest warriors of the Hollowmourne Grand Court charge with devastating ferocity.*

You can re-roll wound rolls of 1 for attacks made with melee weapons by friendly **HOLLOWMOURNE COURTIER** units and friendly **HOLLOWMOURNE KNIGHTS** units that have made a charge move in the same turn.

## COMMAND ABILITY

**Ravenous Crusaders:** *The rulers of the Hollowmourne Grand Court urge their followers ever onwards.*

You can use this command ability at the start of your hero phase. If you do so, pick 1 friendly **HOLLOWMOURNE** unit wholly within 9" of a friendly **HOLLOWMOURNE HERO**, or wholly within 18" of a friendly **HOLLOWMOURNE HERO** that is a general. Add 1 to run and charge rolls for that unit until your next hero phase. In addition, until your next hero phase, that unit can run and still charge later in the same turn.

## COMMAND TRAIT

A **HOLLOWMOURNE** general must have this command trait instead of one listed on page 56.

**Grave Robber:** *The regents of the Hollowmourne Grand Court have sworn a sacred oath to recover the artefacts lost by their emperor centuries ago.*

Add 1 to the Attacks characteristic and Damage characteristic of this general's melee weapons while this general is within 3" of any enemy **HEROES** with an artefact of power.

## ARTEFACT OF POWER

The first **HOLLOWMOURNE HERO** to receive an artefact of power must be given the Corpsefane Gauntlet.

**Corpsefane Gauntlet:** *This glove of decrepit flesh seeps black blood as its wearer charges into battle.*

After this model makes a charge move, you can pick 1 enemy unit within 1" of this model and roll a dice. On a 2+ that enemy unit suffers D3 mortal wounds.

# BLISTERSKIN GRAND COURT

Charred and blistered bodies fill the sky as winged Flesh-eaters of the Blisterskin Grand Court flock to battle. Having risen from the ashes of a sun-worshipping empire, these zealous cannibals now terrorise Aqshy and beyond, leaving trails of devastation in their wake as they spread their twisted beliefs.

With the speed of the screaming desert winds of the Flamescar Plateau, the armies of the Blisterskin Grand Court surge towards their foes. Though they hail from Aqshy, they see the Realm of Light as the most sacred of lands, and in their deranged minds they seek to proselytise their neighbouring kingdoms, preaching the enlightenment of Hysh to all they encounter. Yet in truth they spread only insanity and horror, and instead of imparting wisdom, a visitation by these reeking wretches will see a realm swiftly ground to dust.

In their madness, the Blisterskin royalty still see themselves as priests and priestesses, guiding their faithful subjects in worshipping the Hyshian sun. The most pious mordants and courtiers are gifted with leathery wings with which they can climb high in the sky, allowing them to draw closer to the sun and receive more of its glorious light. Those so blessed are viewed as warrior-saints, and are followed by droves of mordants as they sweep across the lands. Even the mightiest walls cannot hold back the myriad winged cannibals that descend from the skies, and those defenders that are not devoured outright are butchered and left to rot in the blazing heat of the sun. The Blisterskin then move on to their next victims, believing they are leaving behind a city of converts.

## ABILITIES

**Blistering Speed:** *The armies of the Blisterskin Grand Court advance at a terrifying pace.*

Add 2" to the Move characteristic of **BLISTERSKIN** units.

## COMMAND ABILITY

**Lords of the Burning Skies:** *The winged warriors of the Blisterskin Grand Court take to the skies in order to encircle their foes.*

You can use this command ability at the start of your movement phase. If you do so, pick 1 friendly **BLISTERSKIN** unit that can fly and which is wholly within 12" of a friendly **BLISTERSKIN HERO**, or wholly within 18" of a friendly **BLISTERSKIN HERO** that is a general. Remove that unit from the battlefield and then set it up again anywhere on the battlefield more than 9" from any enemy units. It may not move later in that movement phase.

## COMMAND TRAIT

A **BLISTERSKIN** general must have this command trait instead of one listed on page 56.

**Hellish Orator:** *The subjects of the Blisterskin Grand Court blindly follow the divine commands of their rulers.*

If this general is on the battlefield at the start of your hero phase, roll a dice. On a 4+ you receive 1 additional command point.

## ARTEFACT OF POWER

The first **BLISTERSKIN HERO** to receive an artefact of power must be given the Eye of Hysh.

**Eye of Hysh:** *Gouged from the eye socket of a crystal drake, this orb still emits blinding beams of light that fill the mind with visions of horror.*

Subtract 1 from hit rolls for attacks made with missile weapons that target a friendly **BLISTERSKIN** unit wholly within 6" of the bearer.

# GRISTLEGORE GRAND COURT

The bestial Flesh-eaters of the Gristlegore Grand Court started their hunts in Ghur before preying upon lands across other Mortal Realms. In their minds' eye they see themselves as exemplars of tranquillity, but in truth the Gristlegore royalty are savagery made manifest.

The Gristlegore courts were once kingdoms where introspection and finding balance with one's surroundings were the highest of virtues. Amidst the wilderness in the Realm of Beasts, where animals, plants and even the land itself are in constant and savage competition, the peoples of these kingdoms sought peace and harmony. The royal families honed the art of swordplay so that, should violence enter their domains, they could swiftly best any enemy and save their subjects from the horrors of war. But even the peerless martial skill of these royals could not hold back the atrocities of the Age of Chaos, nor the madness that was to follow.

The nobility of the Gristlegore Grand Court still believe themselves to be harbingers of peace, who resort to violence only when absolutely necessary, but this could not be further from reality. Abhorrants and courtiers charge without restraint towards whatever enemies they see, ripping organs from bodies and severing limbs as they thrash at their foes. Where once they would fast for long periods to centre themselves, they now gorge constantly on the meat and bone of those they kill. Packs of mordants sometimes scrabble in their wake, lapping up the blood that spills to the ground, but only the monstrous Zombie Dragons and Terrorgheists are able to match the frenetic pace at which the nobility slaughters.

## ABILITIES

**Peerless Ferocity:** *The champions and great beasts of the Gristlegore Grand Court fight with a savage fury.*

If the unmodified hit roll for an attack made by a **GRISTLEGORE HERO** or **GRISTLEGORE MONSTER** is 6, that attack inflicts 2 hits on that target instead of 1. Make a wound and save roll for each hit.

## COMMAND ABILITY

**Call to War:** *The rulers of the Gristlegore Grand Court can compel their subjects to bursts of horrific violence, even when they are at the verge of death.*

You can use this command ability in the combat phase if a friendly **GRISTLEGORE HERO** or **GRISTLEGORE MONSTER** that has not fought in that phase is slain while it is wholly within 12" of a friendly **GRISTLEGORE HERO**, or wholly within 18" of a friendly **GRISTLEGORE HERO** that is a general. If you do so, before that model is removed from play, it can make a pile-in move and then attack with all of the melee weapons it is armed with. You cannot pick the same unit to benefit from this ability more than once per phase.

## COMMAND TRAIT

A **GRISTLEGORE** general must have this command trait instead of one listed on page 56.

**Savage Strike:** *A Gristlegore abhorrant can overwhelm a foe before they get a chance to fight back.*

This general fights at the start of the combat phase, before the players pick any other units to fight in that combat phase. This general cannot fight again in that combat phase unless an ability or spell allows it to fight more than once.

## ARTEFACT OF POWER

The first **GRISTLEGORE HERO** to receive an artefact of power must be given the Ghurish Mawshard.

**Ghurish Mawshard:** *This splinter of realmstone allows the bearer's jaw to gape wide and devour a victim.*

Once per battle, at the start of the combat phase, you can pick 1 enemy model within 1" of the bearer and roll a dice. If the roll is greater than that model's Wounds characteristic, that model is slain.

# STIRRING THE NEST

Such is the decrepit nature of the lands ruled over by the Abhorrant Ghoul Kings that it is common for armies on the march to be entirely unaware of the danger they are advancing into until it is far too late. As they advance into territory that has seemingly been long abandoned, swarms of Flesh-eaters burst forth from every angle to overwhelm the unwitting invaders.

## THE ARMIES
Each player picks an army as described in the core rules. One player is the Flesh-eater Courts player and their opponent is the Intruder. The Flesh-eater Courts player must use a Flesh-eater Courts army.

Each army has a unique command ability, as follows.

## FLESH-EATER COURTS COMMAND ABILITY
**Encircle the Prey:** *The general clenches their outstretched fist – a simple command that orders their minions to surround their foes and cut off their escape.*

You can use this command ability at the start of your hero phase. If you do so, pick 1 friendly unit wholly within 16" of your general. That unit can run and still charge later in the same turn.

## INTRUDER COMMAND ABILITY
**Force a Passage:** *With a desperate command, the general calls upon their warriors to disengage and attempt to breach a different section of the enemy lines.*

You can use this command ability at the start of your hero phase. If you do so, pick 1 friendly unit wholly within 16" of your general. That unit can retreat and still charge later in the same turn.

## SET-UP
Before setting up, the Flesh-eater Courts player must divide their army into two groups consisting of a roughly equal number of units.

The Intruder sets up their army wholly within their own territory. The Flesh-eater Courts player then sets up all of the units in one of the groups from their army wholly within their own territory. The territories are shown on the map below. The units in the other group are placed to one side as reserves – they arrive as reinforcements during the second battle round as described below.

## FIRST TURN
The Flesh-eater Courts player decides who takes the first turn in the first battle round.

## THE NEST EMPTIED
*The landscape is suddenly filled with the Ghoul King's minions.*

At the end of the Flesh-eater Court player's second movement phase, the Flesh-eater Courts player sets up all of their reserve units wholly within their own territory and more than 6" from enemy models.

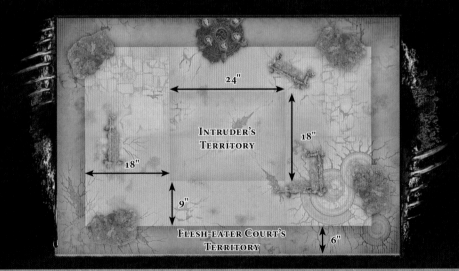

## ESCAPE

*The intruders must break through the Flesh-eater army if they wish to escape.*

At the start of the Intruder's hero phase, and at the end of the fifth battle round, any units from the Intruder's army that are wholly within 6" of the edge of the battlefield and more than 3" from any enemy units can escape the battle. Remove the models in those units from play, but do not count them as being slain.

## GLORIOUS VICTORY

The battle ends at the end of the fifth battle round, or when all the Intruder's units have escaped from the battle or have been destroyed, whichever happens first.

If none of the Intruder's units have escaped from the battle at the end of the game, the Flesh-eater Court's player wins a **major victory**.

If fewer than a third of the Intruder's units (rounding down) have escaped from the battle at the end of the game, the Flesh-eater Court's player wins a **minor victory**.

If more than half of the Intruder's units (rounding down) have escaped from the battle at the end of the game, the Intruder wins a **major victory**.

In any other circumstances, the Intruder wins a **minor victory**.

# PATH TO GLORY

Path to Glory campaigns centre around collecting and fighting battles with a warband in the Age of Sigmar. Champions fight each other and gather followers to join them in their quest for glory, taking advantage of this age of unending battle to win glory and renown.

In order to take part in a Path to Glory campaign, you will need two or more players. All players will need to have at least one **Hero**, who is their champion, and must then create a warband to follow and fight beside their champion during the campaign.

The players fight battles against each other using the warbands they have created. The results of these battles will gain their warband favour. The warband will swell in numbers as more warriors flock to their banner, while existing troops become more powerful.

After gaining enough favour or growing your warband enough to dominate all others through sheer weight of numbers, you will be granted a final test. Succeed, and your glory will be affirmed for all time, and you will be crowned as the victor of the campaign.

## CREATING A WARBAND
When creating a Path to Glory warband, do not select your army in the normal manner. Instead, your army consists of a mighty champion battling to earn the favour of the gods, and their entire band of loyal followers. As you wage war against other warbands, your own warband will grow, and existing units will become grizzled veterans.

### WARBAND ROSTER
The details and progress of each warband need to be recorded on a warband roster, which you can download for free from games-workshop.com.

To create a warband, simply follow these steps and record the results on your warband roster:

1. First, pick an allegiance for your warband. Each allegiance has its own set of warband tables that are used to generate the units

in the warband and the rewards they can receive for fighting battles. The warband tables included in this battletome let you collect a warband with the Flesh-eater Courts allegiance, but other Warhammer Age of Sigmar publications include warband tables to let you collect other warbands from the Grand Alliances of Order, Chaos, Death and Destruction.

2. Next, choose your warband's champion by selecting one of the options from your allegiance's champion table. The champion you choose will determine the number of followers in your warband. Give your champion a suitably grand name, and write this down on your warband roster.

3. Having picked your champion, the next step is to generate your starting followers. These can be chosen from the followers tables for your allegiance. If your allegiance has more than one followers table you can freely choose which ones you use, selecting all of your followers from a single table or from several. Instead of choosing, you can place your destiny in the hands of fate and roll on the followers tables instead. To make a followers roll, pick a column from one of the followers tables and then roll a dice.

4. Your followers need to be organised into units. The follower table tells you how many models the unit has. Follower units cannot include additional models, but they can otherwise take any options listed on their warscroll. Record all of the information about your followers on your warband roster.

5. Instead of generating a unit of followers, your champion can start the campaign with a Champion's

Reward, or one of your units can start with a Follower's Reward. No champion or unit can start the Path to Glory campaign with more than one reward each.

6. Finally, give your warband a name, one that will inspire respect and dread in your rivals. Your warband is now complete, and you can fight your first battle. Good luck!

## TO WAR!
Having created a warband, you can now fight battles with it against other warbands taking part in the campaign. You can fight battles as and when you wish, and can use any of the battleplans available for Warhammer Age of Sigmar.

The units you use for a game must be those on your roster. Units can either be fielded at their full roster strength, or broken down into smaller units, as long as no unit is smaller than the minimum size shown on its pitched battle profile.

Any casualties suffered by a warband are assumed to have been replaced in time for its next battle. If your champion is slain in a battle, it is assumed that they were merely injured, and they are back to full strength for your next game, thirsty for vengeance!

## GAINING GLORY
All of the players in the campaign are vying for glory. The amount of glory they have received is represented by the Glory Points that the warband has accumulated. Glory can be increased by fighting and winning battles, as described next. As a warband's glory increases, it will also attract additional followers, and a warband's champion may be granted rewards.

Warbands receive Glory Points after a battle is complete. If the warband drew or lost the battle, it receives 1 Glory Point. If it won the battle, it receives D3 Glory Points (re-roll a result of 1 if it won a major victory).

Add the Glory Points you scored to the total recorded on your roster. Once you have won 10 Glory Points, you will have a chance to win the campaign, as described below.

## REWARDS OF BATTLE

Each allegiance has its own set of rewards tables. After each battle you can take one of the three following options. Alternatively, roll a D3 to determine which option to take:

**D3   Option**

**1   Additional Followers:** More followers flock to your banner. Either select a new unit or roll for a random one from a follower table, then add it to your warband roster. You can choose from any of your own follower tables, or from any of the follower tables from an allied warband table i.e. a warband table whose allegiance is from the same Grand Alliance as your own. In either case, if you wish to add a unit from a follower table that requires more than '1 roll', you must also reduce your Glory Points total by 1 (if you do not have enough Glory Points, you cannot choose a unit from such a table). Once 5 new units have joined your warband, you will have a chance to win the campaign.

**2   Champion's Reward:** Your champion's prowess grows. Roll on your allegiance's champion rewards table. Note the result on your warband roster. If you roll a result the champion has already received, roll again until you get a different result.

**3   Follower's Reward:** Your warriors become renowned for mighty deeds. Pick a unit of followers (not one from an allied warband table), then roll on your allegiance's followers rewards table. Note the result on your warband roster. If you roll a result the unit has already received, roll again until you get a different result.

## ETERNAL GLORY

There are two ways to win a Path to Glory campaign; either by Blood or by Might. To win by Blood your warband must first have 10 Glory Points. To win by Might your warband must have at least 5 additional units of followers. In either case, you must then fight and win one more battle to win the campaign. If the next battle you fight is tied or lost, you do not receive any Glory Points – just keep on fighting battles until you either win the campaign… or another player wins first!

You can shorten or lengthen a campaign by lowering or raising the number of Glory Points needed to win by Blood, or the number of extra units that must join a warband to win by Might. For example, for a shorter campaign, you could say that a warband only needs 5 Glory Points before the final fight, or for a longer one, say that 15 are needed.

# FLESH-EATER COURTS WARBAND TABLES

Use the following tables to determine the champion that leads your warband, the followers that make up the units which fight at their side, and the rewards they can receive after battle.

## CHAMPION TABLE

| Champion | Followers |
| --- | --- |
| Abhorrant Ghoul King on Royal Terrorgheist or Abhorrant Ghoul King on Royal Zombie Dragon | 1 unit |
| Abhorrant Archregent | 3 units |
| Abhorrant Ghoul King | 4 units |

## RETINUE FOLLOWERS TABLE

| D6 | Followers |
| --- | --- |
| 1-6 | 10 Crypt Ghouls |

## ELITE RETINUE FOLLOWERS TABLE
(uses 2 rolls, or 1 roll and 1 Glory Point)

| D6 | Followers |
| --- | --- |
| 1-3 | 3 Crypt Flayers |
| 4-6 | 3 Crypt Horrors |

## HERO FOLLOWERS TABLE

| D6 | Followers |
| --- | --- |
| 1-2 | Crypt Ghast Courtier |
| 3-4 | Crypt Haunter Courtier |
| 5-6 | Crypt Infernal Courtier |

## MIGHTY HERO FOLLOWERS TABLE
(uses 2 rolls, or 1 roll and 1 Glory Point)

| D6 | Followers |
| --- | --- |
| 1-6 | Varghulf Courtier |

## BEHEMOTH FOLLOWERS TABLE
(uses 3 rolls, or 1 roll and 2 Glory Points)

| D6 | Followers |
| --- | --- |
| 1-3 | Royal Terrorgheist |
| 4-6 | Royal Zombie Dragon |

## FOLLOWERS REWARDS TABLE

**D6  Reward**

**1  King's Own:** *At their lord's command, these loyal followers hurl themselves at the foe.*

In the combat phase, after this unit has fought in that combat phase for the first time, when it is your turn to pick a unit to fight with later in the same combat phase, this unit can be selected to fight for a second time if it is within 3" of any enemy units and within 6" of your champion.

**2  Hungry For Flesh:** *These demented warriors are driven into a ravenous frenzy when they smell blood.*

Once per battle, at the start of the combat phase, you can add 1 to the Attacks characteristic of any melee weapons used by this unit in that combat phase.

**3  Vendetta:** *These followers hold an unshakeable hatred for one of their foes.*

After armies are set up, but before the first battle round begins, pick 1 enemy unit. Add 1 to hit rolls for attacks made by this unit that target that enemy unit.

**4  Gruesome Harvest:** *These warriors display an uncanny talent for acquiring culinary provisions in battle.*

In your hero phase, roll 1 dice for each enemy model within 3" of this unit. For each 6, that model's unit suffers 1 mortal wound.

**5  Fanatical Loyalty:** *These trusted subjects will stand by their lord come what may.*

You can re-roll battleshock tests for this unit.

**6  Martial Excellence:** *These well-drilled mordants fight with iron discipline.*

Once per turn, you can re-roll 1 hit roll or 1 wound roll for an attack made by this unit, or 1 save roll for an attack that targets this unit.

# CHAMPION REWARDS TABLE

**2D6   Reward**

**2    Lord of Darkness:** *An aura of dark power surrounds this champion, empowering nearby courtiers.*

When a friendly **Courtier** within 10" of this champion uses a Muster ability, you can roll 1 extra dice for that **Courtier** when determining how many slain models the Muster ability allows you to return (usually this will mean that you roll 7 dice instead of 6 dice).

**3    Enmity:** *Memories of slights and grievances inspire this champion to commit terrible acts of vengeance.*

At the end of each battle, note down the name of the warband you fought the battle against. Add 1 to hit rolls and wound rolls for attacks made by this champion that target models from that warband for the rest of the campaign.

**4    Terrifying Appearance:** *The appearance of this champion is horrific even for a Flesh-eater.*

Subtract 2 from the Bravery characteristic of enemy units while they are within 6" of this champion.

**5    Arcane Abomination:** *This champion has mastered the arcane arts, and is one of the mightiest spellcasters of his kind.*

Add 1 to casting, dispelling and unbinding rolls for this champion.

**6    Haunted Blade:** *One of the weapons wielded by this champion is a prison for the soul of a champion from the world-that-was.*

Pick one weapon used by this champion. Improve the Rend characteristic of that weapon by 1. This reward has no effect on this model's mount.

**7    Hard to Kill:** *Your champion is able to withstand injuries that would fell a lesser warrior.*

Add 1 to this champion's Wounds characteristic.

**8    Feared Leader:** *The minions that serve under this champion's command have learnt never to disobey his commands.*

Add 1 to the Bravery characteristic of friendly units while they are wholly within 12" of this champion.

**9    Death Incarnate:** *This champion strikes with a savage fury that inflicts terrible wounds.*

You can re-roll wound rolls of 1 for this champion.

**10    Frenzied Charge:** *This champion hurls himself at the foe, his madness lending his attacks incredible speed.*

Add 1 to the Attacks characteristic of this champion's melee weapons until the end of the phase if this champion made a charge move in the same turn. This reward has no effect on this model's mount.

**11    Immortal Fiend:** *This Flesh-eater's polluted blood grants him resilience in battle, allowing him to shrug off serious injuries with ease.*

Once per battle, in your hero phase, you can heal up to D6 wounds allocated to this champion.

**12    Charismatic Fiend:** *This champion's grim regality draws countless cannibalistic warriors to his banner.*

If this champion is chosen as the model that uses a command ability that summons **Flesh-eater Courts** models to the battlefield, they can use it without a command point having to be spent. If they do not have such a command ability, they can use the Summon Men-at-arms ability from the Abhorrant Ghoul King warscroll (pg 79) instead.

# WARSCROLLS

This section includes Flesh-eater Courts warscrolls, warscroll battalions and endless spell warscrolls. Updated February 2019; the warscrolls printed in this book take precedence over any warscrolls with an earlier publication date or no publication date.

## WARSCROLL BATTALION
# CANNIBAL COURT

Upon scenting the fresh meat of an enemy army, an entire court is roused to frenzy. Packs of mordants scrabble behind snarling courtiers, who in turn flock to the maddened howls of the abhorrants, and as one they surge across the land in search of their next gruesome feast.

## ORGANISATION

A Cannibal Court consists of the following warscroll battalions:

- 1 Royal Family
- 1 Attendants at Court
- 1 Deadwatch (pg 74)
- 1 Abattoir (pg 74)
- 1 Ghoul Patrol (pg 74)
- 1 King's Ghouls (pg 75)
- 1 Royal Mordants (pg 75)
- 1 Royal Menagerie (pg 75)

## ABILITIES

**Dark Master:** *The supreme ruler of a court can summon forth minions and sycophants from across his domain at will.*

If your general is an **ABHORRANT ARCHREGENT** or **ABHORRANT GHOUL KING** from this battalion, treat their warscroll as having the command abilities found on the warscrolls of any other units included in this battalion.

# WARSCROLL BATTALION
# ROYAL FAMILY

## ORGANISATION

A Royal Family consists of the following units:

- 1 Abhorrant Archregent, or 1 Abhorrant Ghoul King on Royal Terrorgheist, or 1 Abhorrant Ghoul King on Royal Zombie Dragon

- 2-6 Abhorrant Ghoul Kings

## ABILITIES

**Lords of the Manor**: *In the dominating presence of their royal masters, courtiers of every rank call forth their minions in ever greater numbers.*

When a friendly **COURTIER** within 10" of any models from this battalion uses a Muster ability, you can roll 1 extra dice for that **COURTIER** when determining how many slain models the Muster ability allows you to return (usually this will mean that you roll 7 dice instead of 6 dice).

# WARSCROLL BATTALION
# ATTENDANTS AT COURT

## ORGANISATION

An Attendants at Court battalion consists of the following units:

- 1 Crypt Haunter Courtier

- 2 units of Crypt Horrors

## ABILITIES

**Loyal Subjects**: *The Crypt Horrors known as the Lickspittles are the king's most trusted subjects, and can be relied upon to fight with murderous fury even when they are far from their master's gaze.*

You can re-roll hit rolls for attacks made by models from this battalion if your general is an **ABHORRANT ARCHREGENT** or **ABHORRANT GHOUL KING** and has not been slain.

## WARSCROLL BATTALION
# DEADWATCH

### ORGANISATION

A Deadwatch consists of the following units:

- 1 Crypt Infernal Courtier

- 3 units of Crypt Flayers

### ABILITIES

**The Lord's Own:** *Nominally the king's bodyguard, the winged monstrosities that form the ranks of the Deadwatch epitomise the belief that the best defence is a good offence.*

In your hero phase, 1 unit from this battalion that is within 3" of an enemy unit can make a pile-in move and then attack with all of the melee weapons it is armed with.

## WARSCROLL BATTALION
# ABATTOIR

### ORGANISATION

An Abattoir consists of the following units:

- 1 Crypt Haunter Courtier

- 2 units of Crypt Horrors

- 1 unit of Crypt Ghouls

### ABILITIES

**Body-part Acquisition:** *True to their purpose, the Abattoir displays an uncanny talent for acquiring culinary provisions in battle.*

At the end of the combat phase, roll 1 dice for each enemy model within 3" of any models from this battalion. For each 6, that enemy model's unit suffers 1 mortal wound.

## WARSCROLL BATTALION
# GHOUL PATROL

### ORGANISATION

A Ghoul Patrol consists of the following units:

- 1 Crypt Ghast Courtier

- 3 units of Crypt Ghouls

### ABILITIES

**On Patrol:** *Scuttling through the shadows, the mordants of the Ghoul Patrol burst from the darkness to ambush their prey.*

Instead of setting up a unit from this battalion on the battlefield, you can place it to one side and say that it is on patrol in reserve. At the end of your first movement phase, you must set up all of the units from this battalion that are in reserve. Set up each unit wholly within 6" of the edge of the battlefield and more than 9" from any enemy units.

## WARSCROLL BATTALION
# KING'S GHOULS

### ORGANISATION

A King's Ghouls battalion consists of the following units:

- 1 Crypt Ghast Courtier
- 1 unit of Crypt Horrors
- 2 units of Crypt Ghouls

### ABILITIES

**Guardians of the Court**: *Tasked with protecting the lair of their master, the King's Ghouls would rather fight to the last than see it ransacked by intruders.*

Do not take battleshock tests for units from this battalion while they are wholly within 18" of the Crypt Ghast Courtier from the same battalion.

## WARSCROLL BATTALION
# ROYAL MORDANTS

### ORGANISATION

A Royal Mordants battalion consists of the following units:

- 1 Varghulf Courtier
- 1 unit of Crypt Horrors
- 1 unit of Crypt Flayers
- 1 unit of Crypt Ghouls

### ABILITIES

**Delusional Discipline**: *Well-drilled on parade and instilled with iron discipline – to their deluded minds, at least – the Royal Mordants heed the bestial roars of their courtier without a moment's hesitation.*

In your hero phase, pick 1 unit from this battalion wholly within 16" of the Varghulf Courtier from the same battalion. That unit can make a normal move.

## WARSCROLL BATTALION
# ROYAL MENAGERIE

### ORGANISATION

A Royal Menagerie consists of the following units:

- 3+ Royal Terrorgheists or Royal Zombie Dragons in any combination

### ABILITIES

**Monstrous Ensemble**: *When massed together, the creatures of the Royal Menagerie gain mutual benefit from the dark energies coursing through their vast bodies.*

In your hero phase, you can heal up to D3 wounds allocated to each model from this battalion that is within 5" of any other models from the same battalion.

# ABHORRANT GHOUL KING
## ON ROYAL TERRORGHEIST

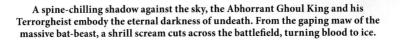

**WOUNDS** 14
**MOVE** ✸
**SAVE** 4+
10
**BRAVERY**

76

A spine-chilling shadow against the sky, the Abhorrant Ghoul King and his Terrorgheist embody the eternal darkness of undeath. From the gaping maw of the massive bat-beast, a shrill scream cuts across the battlefield, turning blood to ice.

| MISSILE WEAPONS | Range | Attacks | To Hit | To Wound | Rend | Damage |
|---|---|---|---|---|---|---|
| Death Shriek | 10" | 1 | See below | | | |
| **MELEE WEAPONS** | **Range** | **Attacks** | **To Hit** | **To Wound** | **Rend** | **Damage** |
| Gory Talons and Fangs | 1" | 5 | 3+ | 3+ | -1 | 1 |
| Skeletal Claws | 2" | ✸ | 4+ | 3+ | -1 | D3 |
| Fanged Maw | 3" | 3 | 4+ | 3+ | -2 | D6 |

| DAMAGE TABLE | | | |
|---|---|---|---|
| Wounds Suffered | Move | Death Shriek | Skeletal Claws |
| 0-3 | 14" | 6 | 4 |
| 4-6 | 12" | 5 | 4 |
| 7-9 | 10" | 4 | 3 |
| 10-12 | 8" | 3 | 3 |
| 13+ | 6" | 2 | 2 |

## DESCRIPTION

An Abhorrant Ghoul King on Royal Terrorgheist is a single model armed with Gory Talons and Fangs.

**MOUNT:** This model's Royal Terrorgheist attacks with its Death Shriek, Skeletal Claws and Fanged Maw.

**FLY:** This model can fly.

## ABILITIES

**Death Shriek:** *The terrifying shriek of a Terrorgheist is enough to stop a warrior's heart.*

Do not use the attack sequence for an attack made with this model's Death Shriek. Instead roll a dice and add the Death Shriek value shown on this model's damage table. If the total is higher than the target unit's Bravery characteristic, the target unit suffers a number of mortal wounds equal to the difference between its Bravery characteristic and the total.

**Gaping Maw:** *This horrific creature bites a great chunk out of its prey, or even swallows it whole.*

If the unmodified hit roll for an attack made with this model's Fanged Maw is 6, that attack inflicts 6 mortal wounds on the target unit and the attack sequence ends (do not make a wound or save roll).

**Infested:** *When a Terrorgheist is finally destroyed, it explodes into a swarm of bats that feast on those nearby.*

If this model is slain, before this model is removed from play each unit within 3" of this model suffers D3 mortal wounds.

**Royal Blood:** *The vampiric blood that courses through a Ghoul King's veins can heal even the most terrible wounds.*

In your hero phase, you can heal up to D3 wounds allocated to this model.

## MAGIC

This model is a **WIZARD**. It can attempt to cast one spell in your hero phase, and attempt to unbind one spell in the enemy hero phase. It knows the Arcane Bolt, Mystic Shield and Unholy Vitality spells.

**Unholy Vitality:** *The Abhorrant Ghoul King infuses the crooked bodies of his minions with dark magic, making it nigh impossible for their enemies to stop their ravenous onslaught.*

Unholy Vitality has a casting value of 6. If successfully cast, pick 1 friendly **FLESH-EATER COURTS** unit wholly within 24" of the caster and visible to them. Until your next hero phase, roll a dice each time you allocate a wound or mortal wound to that unit. On a 5+ that wound or mortal wound is negated.

## COMMAND ABILITIES

**Summon Royal Guard:** *With a snarled command, the Ghoul King calls forth his most elite retainers.*

You can use this command ability at the end of your movement phase. If you do so, pick 1 friendly model that has this command ability and has not used it before in the battle. That model summons 1 unit of up to 3 **KNIGHTS** to the battlefield. The summoned unit is added to your army, and must be set up wholly within 6" of the edge of the battlefield and more than 9" from any enemy units.

| KEYWORDS | DEATH, VAMPIRE, FLESH-EATER COURTS, ABHORRANT, MONSTER, HERO, WIZARD, ABHORRANT GHOUL KING |
|---|---|

*An Abhorrant Ghoul King stands atop his Royal Terrorgheist, the horrifying howls of both rider and mount serving as a clarion call to the courtiers and mordants of the surrounding lands.*

| MOVE |
| SAVE |
| WOUNDS |
| BRAVERY |

14 / 4+ / 10

# ABHORRANT GHOUL KING
## ON ROYAL ZOMBIE DRAGON

Surrounded by an aura of potent dark magic, the Abhorrant Ghoul King and his Zombie Dragon are death incarnate. As the monster shreds foes with fangs the size of swords, the king pulls warriors apart with his bare hands.

| MISSILE WEAPONS | Range | Attacks | To Hit | To Wound | Rend | Damage |
|---|---|---|---|---|---|---|
| Pestilential Breath | 9" | 1 | 3+ | ✱ | -3 | D6 |
| **MELEE WEAPONS** | **Range** | **Attacks** | **To Hit** | **To Wound** | **Rend** | **Damage** |
| Gory Talons and Fangs | 1" | 5 | 3+ | 3+ | -1 | 1 |
| Snapping Maw | 3" | 3 | 4+ | 3+ | -2 | D6 |
| Sword-like Claws | 2" | ✱ | 4+ | 3+ | -1 | 2 |

| DAMAGE TABLE | | | |
|---|---|---|---|
| Wounds Suffered | Move | Pestilential Breath | Sword-like Claws |
| 0-3 | 14" | 2+ | 7 |
| 4-6 | 12" | 3+ | 6 |
| 7-9 | 10" | 4+ | 5 |
| 10-12 | 8" | 5+ | 4 |
| 13+ | 6" | 6+ | 3 |

## DESCRIPTION

An Abhorrant Ghoul King on Royal Zombie Dragon is a single model armed with Gory Talons and Fangs.

**MOUNT:** This model's Royal Zombie Dragon attacks with its Pestilential Breath, a Snapping Maw and Sword-like Claws.

**FLY:** This model can fly.

## ABILITIES

**Pestilential Breath:** *When a Zombie Dragon looses its breath, the killing miasma withers flesh and saps life from the living.*

When you attack with this model's Pestilential Breath, roll a dice before making the hit roll for the attack. If the roll is less than or equal to the number of models in the target unit, the attack scores a hit without needing to make a hit roll.

**Royal Blood:** *The vampiric blood that courses through a Ghoul King's veins can heal even the most terrible wounds.*

In your hero phase, you can heal up to D3 wounds allocated to this model.

## MAGIC

This model is a **WIZARD**. It can attempt to cast one spell in your hero phase, and attempt to unbind one spell in the enemy hero phase. It knows the Arcane Bolt, Mystic Shield and Malefic Hunger spells.

**Malefic Hunger:** *As the Abhorrant Ghoul King imposes his dark will upon his minions, they see a ripe banquet before them and descend upon it with ravening fury.*

Malefic Hunger has a casting value of 6. If successfully cast, until your next hero phase you can re-roll wound rolls for attacks made with melee weapons by friendly **FLESH-EATER COURTS** units wholly within 16" of the caster.

## COMMAND ABILITIES

**Summon Courtier:** *With a keening cry, the Ghoul King summons one of his most loyal servants to join the fray.*

You can use this command ability at the end of your movement phase. If you do so, pick 1 friendly model that has this command ability and has not used it before in the battle. That model summons 1 **COURTIER** unit to the battlefield. The summoned unit is added to your army, and must be set up wholly within 6" of the edge of the battlefield and more than 9" from any enemy units.

| KEYWORDS | DEATH, VAMPIRE, FLESH-EATER COURTS, ABHORRANT, MONSTER, HERO, WIZARD, ABHORRANT GHOUL KING |
|---|---|

# ABHORRANT ARCHREGENT

Archregents are Ghoul Kings that have ruled for hundreds upon hundreds of years and have grown terrifyingly powerful. They are supremely mighty vampiric warrior-kings, and are accustomed to the instant obedience of all around them.

| MELEE WEAPONS | Range | Attacks | To Hit | To Wound | Rend | Damage |
|---|---|---|---|---|---|---|
| Gory Talons and Fangs | 1" | 7 | 3+ | 3+ | -1 | 1 |

## DESCRIPTION

An Abhorrant Archregent is a single model armed with Gory Talons and Fangs.

## ABILITIES

**Imperial Blood:** *An Archregent has an unnatural vitality that heals ghastly wounds in moments.*

In your hero phase, you can heal up to 3 wounds allocated to this model.

## MAGIC

This model is a **Wizard**. It can attempt to cast two spells in your hero phase, and attempt to unbind two spells in the enemy hero phase. It knows the Arcane Bolt, Mystic Shield and Ferocious Hunger spells.

**Ferocious Hunger:** *The Archregent's dark sorcery raises its minions' cravings to still greater heights.*

Ferocious Hunger has a casting value of 6. If successfully cast, pick 1 friendly **Flesh-eater Courts** unit wholly within 24" of the caster and visible to them, and roll a D3. Add the roll to the Attacks characteristic of melee weapons used by that unit until your next hero phase.

## COMMAND ABILITIES

**Summon Imperial Guard:** *With a snap of its fingers, the Archregent summons some of its most trusted warriors to the battlefield.*

You can use this command ability at the end of your movement phase. If you do so, pick 1 friendly model that has this command ability and has not used it before in the battle. That model summons 1 of the following units to the battlefield: 1 **Courtier**; or 1 unit of up to 3 **Knights**; or 1 unit of up to 20 **Serfs**. The summoned unit is added to your army, and must be set up wholly within 6" of the edge of the battlefield and more than 9" from any enemy units.

| KEYWORDS | DEATH, VAMPIRE, FLESH-EATER COURTS, ABHORRANT, HERO, WIZARD, ABHORRANT ARCHREGENT |
|---|---|

---

# ABHORRANT GHOUL KING

On foot, the Abhorrant Ghoul King fights among his infantry. With his necromantic magic, the king imbues his followers with even greater fury, urging them into battle even as he rends apart foes with dripping claws and razor fangs.

| MELEE WEAPONS | Range | Attacks | To Hit | To Wound | Rend | Damage |
|---|---|---|---|---|---|---|
| Gory Talons and Fangs | 1" | 6 | 3+ | 3+ | -1 | 1 |

## DESCRIPTION

An Abhorrant Ghoul King is a single model armed with Gory Talons and Fangs.

## ABILITIES

**Royal Blood:** *The vampiric blood that courses through a Ghoul King's veins can heal even the most terrible wounds.*

In your hero phase, you can heal up to D3 wounds allocated to this model.

## MAGIC

This model is a **Wizard**. It can attempt to cast one spell in your hero phase, and attempt to unbind one spell in the enemy hero phase. It knows the Arcane Bolt, Mystic Shield and Black Hunger spells.

**Black Hunger:** *The Ghoul King invokes a terrifying frenzy in his deranged minions.*

Black Hunger has a casting value of 5. If successfully cast, pick 1 friendly **Flesh-eater Courts** unit wholly within 24" of the caster and visible to them. Add 1 to the Attacks characteristic of melee weapons used by that unit until your next hero phase.

## COMMAND ABILITIES

**Summon Men-at-arms:** *With a curt command, the Ghoul King calls forth his finest men-at-arms.*

You can use this command ability at the end of your movement phase. If you do so, pick 1 friendly model that has this command ability and has not used it before in the battle. That model summons 1 unit of up to 10 **Serfs** to the battlefield. The summoned unit is added to your army, and must be set up wholly within 6" of the edge of the battlefield and more than 9" from any enemy units.

| KEYWORDS | DEATH, VAMPIRE, FLESH-EATER COURTS, ABHORRANT, HERO, WIZARD, ABHORRANT GHOUL KING |
|---|---|

# VARGHULF COURTIER

| MOVE | WOUNDS | SAVE | BRAVERY |
|------|--------|------|---------|
| 10" | 8 | 5+ | 10 |

Blood gushing from its fanged maw and matting its fur, the Varghulf Courtier kills without restrain or reason. Even as enemies are heaped broken at its feet, it looses a piercing howl, calling the warriors of the court to its side.

| MELEE WEAPONS | Range | Attacks | To Hit | To Wound | Rend | Damage |
|---------------|-------|---------|--------|----------|------|--------|
| Immense Claws | 2" | 4 | 3+ | 3+ | -1 | 2 |
| Dagger-like Fangs | 1" | 1 | 3+ | 2+ | -2 | D3 |

## DESCRIPTION

A Varghulf Courtier is a single model armed with Immense Claws and Dagger-like Fangs.

**FLY:** This model can fly.

## ABILITIES

**Muster Royal Household:** *With a cry, the courtier calls forth more of the king's minions.*

In your hero phase, roll 6 dice for each friendly **VARGHULF COURTIER** on the battlefield. For each 2+ you can return 1 slain model to a friendly **SERFS** unit within 10" of that **VARGHULF COURTIER**. For each 5+ you can return 1 slain model to a friendly **KNIGHTS** unit within 10" of that **VARGHULF COURTIER** instead. Slain models can be returned to more than one unit if you wish, but each successful dice roll can only be used to return a model to a single unit.

**Feed on Dark Magic:** *These strange creatures can lap up dark magic from the air.*

If a friendly **ABHORRANT** within 18" of this model successfully casts a spell, and it is not unbound, you can re-roll hit rolls for this model until the start of your next hero phase.

**King's Champion:** *A Varghulf enters a terrifying frenzy when surrounded by foes.*

Add 2 to the Attacks characteristic of this model's Immense Claws if it is within 3" of 10 or more enemy models when you pick the target unit(s) for its attacks.

**Victory Feast:** *When a Varghulf swallows chunks of flesh ripped from its foes, its own wounds disappear.*

At the end of the combat phase, if any enemy models were slain by wounds inflicted by this model's attacks in that combat phase, you can heal up to D3 wounds allocated to this model.

| KEYWORDS | DEATH, MORDANT, FLESH-EATER COURTS, COURTIER, HERO, VARGHULF COURTIER |
|----------|----------------------------------------------------------------------|

*The bestial howls of a Hollowmourne Varghulf Courtier echo through the rubble of a dead civilisation, yet in the monstrous cannibal's mind it is standing proud atop the walls of a mighty citadel, ready to defend the king and his subjects.*

# CRYPT GHAST COURTIER

Hissing captains of the mordants, Crypt Ghast Courtiers move among the pale ranks of the king's army to direct the cannibal formations. They drive more Ghouls into the fray, while seeking out gruesome trophies to bestow upon their 'men'.

| MELEE WEAPONS | Range | Attacks | To Hit | To Wound | Rend | Damage |
|---|---|---|---|---|---|---|
| Bone Club | 1" | 3 | 3+ | 3+ | - | 1 |
| Filthy Claws | 1" | 2 | 4+ | 3+ | - | 1 |

## DESCRIPTION

A Crypt Ghast Courtier is a single model armed with a Bone Club and Filthy Claws.

## ABILITIES

**Muster Serfs:** *With a cry, the courtier calls forth more of the Ghoul King's lowest minions.*

In your hero phase, roll 6 dice for each friendly **CRYPT GHAST COURTIER** on the battlefield. For each 2+ you can return 1 slain model to a friendly **SERFS** unit that is within 10" of that **CRYPT GHAST COURTIER**. Slain models can be returned to more than one unit if you wish, but each successful dice roll can only be used to return a model to a single unit.

**Trophy Hunter:** *Crypt Ghast Courtiers inspire their followers by holding aloft trophies torn from the bodies of their slain foes.*

If any enemy models are slain by wounds inflicted by this model's attacks, until the end of the phase in which the attacks were made add 1 to the Attacks characteristic of melee weapons used by friendly **SERFS** units while they are wholly within 16" of this model.

| KEYWORDS | DEATH, MORDANT, FLESH-EATER COURTS, COURTIER, HERO, CRYPT GHAST COURTIER |
|---|---|

# CRYPT GHOULS

Filled with a dark hunger, Crypt Ghouls pounce upon their prey. They are ferocious in great numbers, as each mordant competes with its kin for food. Should a ghoul catch a glimpse of their king, they will fight all the harder, eager to prove their worth.

| MELEE WEAPONS | Range | Attacks | To Hit | To Wound | Rend | Damage |
|---|---|---|---|---|---|---|
| Sharpened Teeth and Filthy Claws | 1" | 2 | 4+ | 4+ | - | 1 |

## DESCRIPTION

A unit of Crypt Ghouls has any number of models, each armed with Sharpened Teeth and Filthy Claws.

**CRYPT GHAST:** The leader of this unit is a Crypt Ghast. Add 1 to the Attacks characteristic of a Crypt Ghast's Sharpened Teeth and Filthy Claws.

## ABILITIES

**Boundless Ferocity:** *When Crypt Ghouls gather in large numbers their ferocity knows no bounds.*

Add 1 to the Attacks characteristic of this unit's Sharpened Teeth and Filthy Claws while this unit has 20 or more models.

**Royal Approval:** *Crypt Ghouls will always do their utmost to attract the attention of their sovereign.*

You can re-roll hit rolls of 1 for attacks made by this unit while it is wholly within 18" of any friendly **ABHORRANTS**.

| KEYWORDS | DEATH, MORDANT, FLESH-EATER COURTS, SERFS, CRYPT GHOULS |
|---|---|

**82**

MOVE **12"**

WOUNDS **6**

SAVE **4+**

BRAVERY **10**

# CRYPT INFERNAL COURTIER

Leathery wings tucked against its body, the Crypt Infernal Courtier dives down from the sky, shrieking its rage. Plunging into the midst of its enemies with killing force, the vicious beast impales its prey in a shower of steaming gore.

| MISSILE WEAPONS | Range | Attacks | To Hit | To Wound | Rend | Damage |
|---|---|---|---|---|---|---|
| Foetid Breath | 9" | 1 | 4+ | 3+ | -1 | D3 |
| MELEE WEAPONS | Range | Attacks | To Hit | To Wound | Rend | Damage |
| Skewering Talons | 1" | 5 | 4+ | 3+ | -1 | 2 |

## DESCRIPTION

A Crypt Infernal Courtier is a single model armed with Foetid Breath and Skewering Talons.

**FLY:** This model can fly.

## ABILITIES

**Skewering Strike:** *Sometimes a Crypt Infernal Courtier will strike with such force that the victim is skewered upon its piercing talons.*

If the unmodified hit roll for an attack made with Skewering Talons is 6, that attack inflicts 1 mortal wound on the target in addition to any normal damage.

**Muster Royal Guard:** *With a cry, the courtier calls forth more of the Ghoul King's minions.*

In your hero phase, roll 6 dice for each friendly **CRYPT INFERNAL COURTIER** on the battlefield. For each 5+ you can return 1 slain model to a friendly **CRYPT FLAYERS** unit that is within 10" of that **CRYPT INFERNAL COURTIER**. Slain models can be returned to more than one unit if you wish, but each successful dice roll can only be used to return a model to a single unit.

**KEYWORDS** | DEATH, MORDANT, FLESH-EATER COURTS, COURTIER, HERO, CRYPT INFERNAL COURTIER

---

MOVE **12"**

WOUNDS **4**

SAVE **5+**

BRAVERY **10**

# CRYPT FLAYERS

Monstrous predators of the sky, Crypt Flayers flock together in a beating of dark wings and hissing maws. Enemies are snatched up by their sudden strikes and torn asunder while the creatures' keening call is enough to break a warrior's spirit.

| MISSILE WEAPONS | Range | Attacks | To Hit | To Wound | Rend | Damage |
|---|---|---|---|---|---|---|
| Death Scream | 10" | 1 | — See below — | | | |
| MELEE WEAPONS | Range | Attacks | To Hit | To Wound | Rend | Damage |
| Piercing Talons | 1" | 4 | 4+ | 3+ | -1 | 1 |

## DESCRIPTION

A unit of Crypt Flayers has any number of models, each armed with a Death Scream and Piercing Talons.

**CRYPT INFERNAL:** The leader of this unit is a Crypt Infernal. Add 1 to the Attacks characteristic of a Crypt Infernal's Piercing Talons.

**FLY:** This unit can fly.

## ABILITIES

**Death Scream:** *Crypt Flayers can unleash an ultrasonic cry that can kill or debilitate their victims.*

Do not use the attack sequence for an attack made with a Death Scream. Instead roll 2D6. Subtract 2 if the target unit is more than 3" from the attacking model. If the result is higher than the target unit's Bravery characteristic, the target unit suffers a number of mortal wounds equal to the difference between its Bravery characteristic and the result.

**Skewering Strike:** *Sometimes a Crypt Flayer will strike with such force that the victim is skewered upon its piercing talons.*

If the unmodified hit roll for an attack made with Piercing Talons is 6, that attack inflicts 1 mortal wound on the target in addition to any normal damage.

**KEYWORDS** | DEATH, MORDANT, FLESH-EATER COURTS, KNIGHTS, CRYPT FLAYERS

MOVE **7"**

WOUNDS **6**

SAVE **4+**

BRAVERY **10**

# CRYPT HAUNTER COURTIER

A Crypt Haunter Courtier charges into the fray to the sound of ripping flesh and splintering bones. Broken and battered, their foes die by the dozen, even as the carrion knight's own misshapen body knits itself back together again with terrifying speed.

| MELEE WEAPONS | Range | Attacks | To Hit | To Wound | Rend | Damage |
|---|---|---|---|---|---|---|
| Massive Bone Club | 1" | 3 | 4+ | 3+ | - | 3 |
| Rancid Talons | 1" | 2 | 4+ | 3+ | - | 1 |

## DESCRIPTION

A Crypt Haunter Courtier is a single model armed with a Massive Bone Club and Rancid Talons.

## ABILITIES

**Noble Blood:** *The blood of their liege grants Crypt Haunter Courtiers a supernatural ability to heal any damage they suffer.*

In your hero phase, you can heal 1 wound allocated to this model.

**Chosen of the King:** *Crypt Haunters are amongst the most ardent of courtiers.*

You can re-roll hit rolls for attacks made by this model while it is within 18" of any friendly **ABHORRANTS**.

**Muster King's Chosen:** *With a cry, the courtier calls forth more of the Ghoul King's minions.*

In your hero phase, roll 6 dice for each friendly **CRYPT HAUNTER COURTIER** on the battlefield. For each 5+ you can return 1 slain model to a friendly **CRYPT HORRORS** unit that is within 10" of that **CRYPT HAUNTER COURTIER**. Slain models can be returned to more than one unit if you wish, but each successful dice roll can only be used to return a model to a single unit.

| KEYWORDS | DEATH, MORDANT, FLESH-EATER COURTS, COURTIER, HERO, CRYPT HAUNTER COURTIER |
|---|---|

---

MOVE **7"**

WOUNDS **4**

SAVE **5+**

BRAVERY **10**

# CRYPT HORRORS

Each sweep of a Crypt Horror's claws ladles heaps of dripping meat into its gaping maw. Blessed by the abhorrant's blood, their own flesh heals quickly, and even mortal wounds close over as if they never were.

| MELEE WEAPONS | Range | Attacks | To Hit | To Wound | Rend | Damage |
|---|---|---|---|---|---|---|
| Club and Septic Talons | 1" | 3 | 4+ | 3+ | - | 2 |

## DESCRIPTION

A unit of Crypt Horrors has any number of models, each armed with a Club and Septic Talons.

**CRYPT HAUNTER:** The leader of this unit is a Crypt Haunter. Add 1 to the Attacks characteristic of a Crypt Haunter's Club and Septic Talons.

## ABILITIES

**Chosen of the King:** *Crypt Horrors are the most devoted servants in a Ghoul King's army.*

You can re-roll hit rolls for attacks made by this unit while it is wholly within 18" of any friendly **ABHORRANT**.

**Noble Blood:** *The blood of their liege grants Crypt Horrors a supernatural ability to heal any damage that they suffer.*

In your hero phase, you can heal 1 wound allocated to this unit.

**Warrior Elite:** *Crypt Horrors are amongst the most deadly warriors in a court.*

If the unmodified wound roll for an attack made with a Club and Septic Talons is 6, that attack has a Damage characteristic of 3 instead of 2.

| KEYWORDS | DEATH, MORDANT, FLESH-EATER COURTS, KNIGHTS, CRYPT HORRORS |
|---|---|

| | |
|---|---|
| MOVE | |
| 14 | 4+ SAVE |
| 10 | |
| WOUNDS | BRAVERY |

# ROYAL TERRORGHEIST

The Terrorgheist is a bloodthirsty undead beast whose piercing cry scythes through the enemy as it plunges into the fray. Should the creature be slain, another horror awaits its foes, as hundreds of shrieking bats burst from its remains to ravage those nearby.

| MISSILE WEAPONS | Range | Attacks | To Hit | To Wound | Rend | Damage |
|---|---|---|---|---|---|---|
| Death Shriek | 10" | 1 | | See below | | |
| **MELEE WEAPONS** | **Range** | **Attacks** | **To Hit** | **To Wound** | **Rend** | **Damage** |
| Skeletal Claws | 2" | ✹ | 4+ | 3+ | -1 | D3 |
| Fanged Maw | 3" | 3 | 4+ | 3+ | -2 | D6 |

| DAMAGE TABLE | | | |
|---|---|---|---|
| Wounds Suffered | Move | Death Shriek | Skeletal Claws |
| 0-3 | 14" | 6 | 4 |
| 4-6 | 12" | 5 | 4 |
| 7-9 | 10" | 4 | 3 |
| 10-12 | 8" | 3 | 3 |
| 13+ | 6" | 2 | 2 |

## DESCRIPTION

A Royal Terrorgheist is a single model armed with a Death Shriek, Fanged Maw and Skeletal Claws.

**FLY:** This model can fly.

## ABILITIES

**Death Shriek:** *The terrifying shriek of a Terrorgheist is enough to stop a warrior's heart.*

Do not use the attack sequence for an attack made with this model's Death Shriek. Instead roll a dice and add the Death Shriek value shown on this model's damage table. If the total is higher than the target unit's Bravery characteristic, the target unit suffers a number of mortal wounds equal to the difference between its Bravery characteristic and the total.

**Gaping Maw:** *This horrific creature bites a great chunk out of its prey, or even swallows it whole.*

If the unmodified hit roll for an attack made with this model's Fanged Maw is 6, that attack inflicts 6 mortal wounds on the target unit and the attack sequence ends (do not make a wound or save roll).

**Infested:** *When a Terrorgheist is finally destroyed, it explodes into a swarm of bats that feast on those nearby.*

If this model is slain, before this model is removed from play each unit within 3" of this model suffers D3 mortal wounds.

**Royal Menagerie:** *A Royal Terrorgheist's decrepit flesh seethes with dark magic, and reknits as the beast slaughters its way across the battlefield.*

In your hero phase, you can heal up to D3 wounds allocated to this model if this model is within 6" of a friendly **ABHORRANT**.

| KEYWORDS | DEATH, FLESH-EATER COURTS, MENAGERIE, MONSTER, ROYAL TERRORGHEIST |
|---|---|

# ROYAL ZOMBIE DRAGON

**MOVE** ☀
**WOUNDS** 14
**SAVE** 4+
**BRAVERY** 10

With a deafening roar, the Zombie Dragon dives into battle, eye sockets aglow with necromantic energy. The beast shreds flesh, bone and steel with equal ease, its talons and maw matched in their lethality only by its billowing pestilential breath.

| MISSILE WEAPONS | Range | Attacks | To Hit | To Wound | Rend | Damage |
|---|---|---|---|---|---|---|
| Pestilential Breath | 9" | 1 | 3+ | ☀ | -3 | D6 |
| **MELEE WEAPONS** | **Range** | **Attacks** | **To Hit** | **To Wound** | **Rend** | **Damage** |
| Snapping Maw | 3" | 3 | 4+ | 3+ | -2 | D6 |
| Sword-like Claws | 2" | ☀ | 4+ | 3+ | -1 | 2 |

| DAMAGE TABLE | | | |
|---|---|---|---|
| Wounds Suffered | Move | Pestilential Breath | Sword-like Claws |
| 0-3 | 14" | 2+ | 7 |
| 4-6 | 12" | 3+ | 6 |
| 7-9 | 10" | 4+ | 5 |
| 10-12 | 8" | 5+ | 4 |
| 13+ | 6" | 6+ | 3 |

## DESCRIPTION

A Royal Zombie Dragon is a single model armed with Pestilential Breath, a Snapping Maw and Sword-like Claws.

**FLY:** This model can fly.

## ABILITIES

**Pestilential Breath:** *When a Zombie Dragon looses its breath, the killing miasma withers flesh and saps life from the living.*

When you attack with this model's Pestilential Breath, roll a dice before making the hit roll for the attack. If the roll is less than or equal to the number of models in the target unit, the attack scores a hit without needing to make a hit roll.

| KEYWORDS | DEATH, FLESH-EATER COURTS, MENAGERIE, MONSTER, ROYAL ZOMBIE DRAGON |
|---|---|

● ENDLESS SPELL WARSCROLL ●

# CADAVEROUS BARRICADE

*With a word of command the buried dead are brought writhing to the surface. The corpses of those who once served Ushoran rise up from the grave, dragging with them the detritus of their forgotten civilisation, and with lifeless hands they claw at the living who draw too near.*

## DESCRIPTION

A Cadaverous Barricade is a single model.

## MAGIC

**Summon Cadaverous Barricade:** *The wizard snaps a fallen branch in half and hurls it to the ground. In moments it sprouts into a horrific bulwark.*

Summon Cadaverous Barricade has a casting value of 5. Only Nagash, Supreme Lord of the Undead and **ABHORRANTS** can attempt to cast this spell. If successfully cast, set up a Cadaverous Barricade model wholly within 24" of the caster and more than 1" from any enemy units.

## ABILITIES

**Grasping Hands:** *The animated corpses trapped in a Cadaverous Barricade grab at any living creature that approaches too closely.*

If a model starts a move within 3" of this model, halve the distance that model can move when it makes that move. **DEATH** units are not affected by this ability.

**Grisly Obstacle:** *Creatures that are desperate enough can find cover behind a Cadaverous Barricade.*

When a missile weapon targets a unit that has all of its models within 1" of this model, then the target unit receives the benefit of cover if the attacking model is closer to this model than it is to the target unit.

| KEYWORDS | ENDLESS SPELL, SHYISH, CADAVEROUS BARRICADE |
| --- | --- |

● ENDLESS SPELL WARSCROLL ●

# CHALICE OF USHORAN

*Believed to be a manifestation of the sacred cup held by Ushoran, this bone-wrought goblet is continually filled with the blood of those slain in its presence. When the gore inside overflows, the Flesh-eaters upon whom it slops are bestowed with unnatural vitality, their most grievous wounds healing and their dead rising to fight once more.*

## DESCRIPTION

A Chalice of Ushoran is a single model.

## MAGIC

**Summon Chalice of Ushoran:** *The abhorrant conjures forth an ensorcelled chalice of bone from which his raving subjects can sup.*

Summon Chalice of Ushoran has a casting value of 6. Only Nagash, Supreme Lord of the Undead and **ABHORRANTS** can attempt to cast this spell. If successfully cast, set up a Chalice of Ushoran model wholly within 24" of the caster.

## ABILITIES

**Soul Stealer:** *When a creature falls in battle, their screaming essence is trapped by the Chalice of Ushoran, and can be used to heal the wounds suffered by nearby Flesh-eaters.*

Keep track of the number of models that are slain within 12" of this model each turn. At the end of each turn, roll a dice for each model that was slain within 12" of this model during that turn. For each 4+ heal 1 wound allocated to 1 **FLESH-EATER COURTS** model within 12" of this model, or return 1 slain model to 1 **FLESH-EATER COURTS** unit with a Wounds characteristic of 1 that is wholly within 12" of this model.

| KEYWORDS | ENDLESS SPELL, SHYISH, CHALICE OF USHORAN |
| --- | --- |

# CORPSEMARE STAMPEDE

*Imparted with grisly vigour by the insane magics of the abhorrants, the undead beasts of a Corpsemare Stampede burst from the blood-soaked ground. Once loosed they trample across the battlefield with reckless abandon, crushing any foolish enough to be caught in their path.*

## DESCRIPTION

A Corpsemare Stampede is a single model.

**PREDATORY:** A Corpsemare Stampede is a predatory endless spell. It can move up to 14" and can fly.

## MAGIC

**Summon Corpsemare Stampede:** *The wizard hurls a rusty horseshoe. Where it lands, a herd of ferocious ghostly horses spring forth from the ground.*

Summon Corpsemare Stampede has a casting value of 7. Only Nagash, Supreme Lord of the Undead and **ABHORRANTS** can attempt to cast this spell. If successfully cast, set up a Corpsemare Stampede model wholly within 3D6" of the caster.

## ABILITIES

**Crazed Gallop:** *When a Corpsemare Stampede is called forth, it immediately gallops furiously across the battlefield.*

When this model is set up, the player who set it up can immediately make a move with it.

**Trampled Underfoot:** *As a Corpsemare Stampede charges across the battlefield, it tramples over anyone that gets in its way.*

After this model has moved, roll 5 dice for each unit that has any models it passed across. For each roll that is more than that unit's Wounds characteristic, that unit suffers 1 mortal wound. For each roll of 6, that unit suffers D3 mortal wounds instead (whatever its Wounds characteristic is).

| KEYWORDS | ENDLESS SPELL, SHYISH, CORPSEMARE STAMPEDE |
|---|---|

*The death magic of the Flesh-eater Courts is augmented by the madness of the abhorrants who wield it. The Corpsemare Stampede, Chalice of Ushoran and Cadaverous Barricade are amongst the most powerful manifestations of this insanity.*

# PITCHED BATTLE PROFILES

The table below provides points, minimum unit sizes and battlefield roles for the warscrolls and warscroll battalions in this book, for use in Pitched Battles. Spending the points listed on this table allows you to take a minimum-sized unit with any of its upgrades. Understrength units cost the full amount of points. Larger units are taken in multiples of their minimum unit size; multiply their cost by the same amount as you multiplied their size. If a unit has two points values separated by a slash (e.g. '60/200'), the second value is for a maximum sized unit. Units that are listed as 'Unique' are named characters and can only be taken once in an army. A unit that has any of the keywords listed on the Allies table on its warscroll can be taken as an allied unit by a Flesh-eater Courts army. Updated February 2019; the profiles printed here take precedence over any profiles with an earlier publication date or no publication date.

| FLESH-EATER COURTS WARSCROLL | UNIT SIZE MIN | UNIT SIZE MAX | POINTS | BATTLEFIELD ROLE | NOTES |
|---|---|---|---|---|---|
| Crypt Ghouls | 10 | 40 | 100/360 | Battleline | |
| Royal Terrorgheist | 1 | 1 | 300 | Behemoth | Battleline if **GRISTLEGORE** |
| Royal Zombie Dragon | 1 | 1 | 300 | Behemoth | Battleline if **GRISTLEGORE** |
| Abhorrant Archregent | 1 | 1 | 200 | Leader | |
| Abhorrant Ghoul King | 1 | 1 | 140 | Leader | |
| Crypt Ghast Courtier | 1 | 1 | 60 | Leader | |
| Crypt Haunter Courtier | 1 | 1 | 120 | Leader | |
| Crypt Infernal Courtier | 1 | 1 | 120 | Leader | |
| Varghulf Courtier | 1 | 1 | 160 | Leader | |
| Abhorrant Ghoul King on Royal Terrorgheist | 1 | 1 | 400 | Leader, Behemoth | |
| Abhorrant Ghoul King on Royal Zombie Dragon | 1 | 1 | 440 | Leader, Behemoth | |
| Crypt Flayers | 3 | 12 | 170 | | Battleline if general is Crypt Infernal Courtier, or if Crypt Flayers unit is **BLISTERSKIN** |
| Crypt Horrors | 3 | 12 | 160 | | Battleline if general is Crypt Haunter Courtier, or if Crypt Horrors unit is **HOLLOWMOURNE** |
| *Abattoir* | - | - | 120 | *Warscroll Battalion* | |
| *Attendants at Court* | - | - | 110 | *Warscroll Battalion* | |
| *Cannibal Court* | - | - | 60 | *Warscroll Battalion* | |
| *Deadwatch* | - | - | 110 | *Warscroll Battalion* | |
| *Ghoul Patrol* | - | - | 180 | *Warscroll Battalion* | |
| *King's Ghouls* | - | - | 120 | *Warscroll Battalion* | |
| *Royal Family* | - | - | 120 | *Warscroll Battalion* | |
| *Royal Menagerie* | - | - | 120 | *Warscroll Battalion* | |
| *Royal Mordants* | - | - | 120 | *Warscroll Battalion* | |
| *Cadaverous Barricade* | 1 | 1 | 30 | *Endless Spell* | |
| *Chalice of Ushoran* | 1 | 1 | 40 | *Endless Spell* | |
| *Corpsemare Stampede* | 1 | 1 | 60 | *Endless Spell* | |
| *Charnel Throne* | 1 | 1 | 0 | *Scenery* | |

| DEATH | ALLIES |
|---|---|
| Flesh-eater Courts | Deadwalkers, Deathlords, Deathmages |